From the Couch
TO THE STAGE

Strategies to Go from Viewing to Doing

Sara Burton

Published by: Kainos Enterprises
                  7777 Churchville Road
                  Brampton ON Canada L6Y 0H3
                  www.ToTheStage.info

ISBN: 978-1466457010

CONTENTS

Dedication 5
TidBook 6
Introduction...8
1. Entertain Me! 10
2. Dragged down the Road...12
3. It Ain't about the Fish Food 14
4. Starting the Engine..16
5. Hit the Ball to Me! 18
6. The Fear of the Third 20
7. The Critic Trap..22
8. To Swing or Not to Swing..24
9. Get on the Right Track...26
10. Daisy Picking Days..28
11. Put the Bumpers in the Gutter...30
12. Getting the Get up and Go 32
13. Just Add Water 34
14. Cars and Toys..36
15. Using Carrots 38
16. Hurricanes in the House...40
17. I Need a Coffee 42
18. Good Learning from a Bad Book..44
19. Polish the Silver 46
20. Use the Furniture Path 48
21. Reach and Relax 50
22. Gazebo Woes...52
23. Journey of a Thousand Miles 54
24. And on the Seventh Day… 56
25. Rainbow Promises 58
26. Don't Look at the Ball 60
27. The Motivation Muscle..62
28. Opening the Gym Door...64

29. Triple Spill 66
30. Mind Rehearsals..68
31. I Was the Queen of Excuses......................................70
32. It's Not Just about the Scale.....................................72
33. Mama Needs a New Pair of Shoes! 74
34. Lessons from Potty Training.....................................76
35. Pushing to Find Purpose 78
36. Taking the Fitness Stage 80
37. Double Lung Transplant and Still Going....................82
38. How Do I Get Rid of This?..84
39. Participation Obstacles..86
40. Please Don't Make Me Change! 88
41. I Need New Knees!...90
42. Freakishly Long Arms...92
43. Double Stroller Challenge...94
44. Mulligan Lessons..96
45. Destined to Fail? 98
46. How to Look Good – Pregnant!................................100
47. The Pen Is Mightier Than the Sword 102
48. Turning up the Heat 104
49. Ten Way to Go's!..106
50. Up and Down 108
51. Your Destiny 110
52. The Humble Guitar 112

DEDICATION

This book is dedicated to my family and friends. May you continually be inspired to live your greatest life on your very own stage wherever your stage may be..

TIDBOOK

This book is created in the new TidBook format. You may have been encouraged to see the book is rather thin. It is. But the full book is not here in print. This is only half of a book – just a tidbit of the full book. The other parts are on the Internet.

In the Internet portion of "From the Couch to the Stage" there is additional text, audio files, videos, worksheets, thoughtful questions and additional ideas from users. On and on it goes because this is a continual work in progress. Since the subject matter is so important we wanted you to get everything you needed.

There are several advantages to this format. You will immediately recognize that each chapter is only two pages long. That should be enough to get you to focus on the chapter for a bit. Then if you need to drill down to strike oil in one place or another you can. You don't have to wade through all the information that is less relevant to your situation.

If you come across some chapter where you wish there was more all you need to do is go to the Internet page and ask for it and if I possibly can I will find the information you need for you or create it.

I welcome you to submit your success stories with any of the concepts here and I will selectively publish your story in those online resources.

Now the only question is, "How will I get these extras?" First off, if you purchased the book you purchased the other material with it already.

You will notice a QR code at the bottom of each chapter. This is a kind of bar code potentially containing much more information than the older form of bar code. You can download a free QR code reader for your smart phone. To find a reader for your phone, go to your favourite web browser and search for "free QR code reader for [model of your phone]". Download the app to your phone and simply take a picture of the QR code. It usually does this automatically when you get the code in focus. That will immediately send you to the Internet to the page you need.

If you are old school and willing to take another step, you will need to type in the url which is also included. It is in the form www.bit. ly/[extension].

Each chapter is independent. You will only find one chapter at a time. In other words, you can't look at all the resources at once. If you want to view things on your main computer simply send an email to yourself with the page link and then go to your computer to view things at full size.

Now, let's get started together!

INTRODUCTION

What do you call your favourite spot to chill out? The couch? Sofa, chesterfield, lounge, daybed, chaise, loveseat, settee, sectional, recliner, lazy boy, rocker?

The stuffing is a little, shall we say, depleted on the corner of the couch where I sit. The leather is wearing where I lounge.

When I sit I am a viewer. That's what I do. I watch TV and often fall asleep.

I gotta say it's one of my favourite places to be.

Give me a Tim Horton's coffee and perhaps an apple fritter and I'm a happy girl.

I'm sure you don't need encouragement on how to enjoy a comfortable couch in the evening. You know how to be a viewer. That comes naturally, doesn't it?

Check out the prices of advertising on TV and with a little understanding of economics we know that people are sitting somewhere viewing often enough that it makes business sense to present the sales pitch in that medium.

Sometimes I know that I must take a break from my life and just sit. And then there are times when once I've done that I no longer want to move even though I know I should.

Have you ever felt stuck to your couch like that?

From the comfortable place I watch those singers compete on American Idol, brave weekend warriors attempt renovations and sometimes I'll check out one of those weight loss programs where the contestants lose almost half of their body weight.

It's fun to watch. But will those be the best hours of my life? On the last day of my life will I regret having missed the finale of season ten of Dancing with the Stars? If the closest I get to the stage is via a remote control then I wonder if I'm getting the absolute best view.

In fact I have found myself on a few stages in my life mic'd up and eyes on me. And those times that I've stepped off the stage I've noticed that I continue to live on some kind of a stage no matter where I am. Whether it's only one that is watching or an audience of thousands, others notice even when we try to be invisible. People want to see you do something interesting. They do love to see you at your best. When you are not quite there the audience shifts focus and the only person that really loses out is you. It's not that you need an audience but there is an exhilaration that comes with living your best life. Owning the stage gets noticed.

The trick is to get off the couch and live on your own stage. Here is a collection of my stories from the couch to the stage. It is my hope you will enjoy these and perhaps find inspiration to own your very own stage a little more frequently.

• •

The bee that makes the honey doesn't hang around the hive.

• •

http://bit.ly/obDfqc

1. ENTERTAIN ME!

Strategy: Experience inspiration in exposure.

Who doesn't like a good show? Whether we are in the comfort of our own home in front of a big screen TV or dressed to the nines on the town for some live event, we love to be entertained.

Do we not imagine ourselves as the character experiencing the ups and downs, agonies and triumphs? Are we not impressed by the skill or those memorable moments that grab our emotions?

Recently my husband and I attended the Trans-Siberian Orchestra. That was a show. This rock opera takes creativity and performance to a new level. Pyrotechnics, theatre and musical mastery is all there. We got to appreciate the benefit of the production for the relatively small price of a seat; a mutually beneficial arrangement I'm sure. The passion put in we could not miss.

But when it's over we're on to the next show. With a click of a button we might find ourselves in front of something more mediocre. But we feel powerful having the choice.

Funny, isn't it? We have the power of choice of entertainment.

Somehow we are never satisfied and keep flipping the stations. Even when the show is amazing it is quickly forgotten and we're on the prowl for the next latest and greatest.

I wonder what sets us up for this? Is it habit? Is it lack of something else to do? Is it lack of motivation or inspiration?

What inspires you the most from what you watch? What would it take for you to start on a journey in that direction? If you love the rock opera, have you ever picked up a guitar?

Believe me when I tell you – you will suck at the beginning. Even though it looks easy those first hours of learning are painful. It's like taking the first ten steps up the mountain and feeling it is going to be impossible. You look up towards the top and think you won't ever get there.

But without inspiration why would we start? The dream may be so far away but that's okay, isn't it? Taking a first step at least gets us off the couch. Purchasing a ticket to watch from a different venue may also be a first step.

I have only climbed one mountain in my life. It was Mount Fuji in Japan. Take a look at that mountain from a distance it is a beautifully symmetrical giant that can be seen from miles away. When I lived in Tokyo, Japan, my friend pointed out that we could see the mountain from the train near our neighbourhood. On the way to work we had about a ten second chance to take a peak through the buildings at the mountain on a clear day. I would be sure to look for it if I thought there was a chance to see it. Often there were clouds or too much smog; however on the cooler days it was an inspiration.

I'm sure I would never have thought to take a trip to the top of this mountain if it weren't for my friend pointing out the view. I had to see that it was there – even if it were only for a moment as the train whizzed by. I had to see the opportunity and be inspired. To this day, climbing Mount Fuji is one of the highlights of my life. For as much inspiration as I received from looking at the mountain from afar, being at the top for sunrise was awe inspiring.

••

Grass at eye level is taller than the trees half a mile away.

••

http://bit.ly/mRavzN

2. DRAGGED DOWN THE ROAD

Strategy: Let yourself be dragged into something good you wouldn't start alone.

There are many things I have done in my life I might not have done if I didn't have someone with me. I spent some time teaching English in Japan and had a wonderful experience for three years. When I think back to how I made that decision it was not alone. I never would have gone if friends didn't first find out about it and encourage us to come along. As it turned out, we flew over together and parted ways when we went to our new apartments. Although we tried to keep in contact, we lived just too far away from each other to make regular visits convenient. In the end we never did hear how long they stayed in Japan but thanks to them we went and had one of the best times of our lives.

On another occasion before I started exercising regularly a friend asked me to get a membership at a gym with her. There was some two for one special and she insisted that she would pay for the whole thing as long as I would just go with her and be her workout buddy. How could I say no to that? We had lots of fun chatting away on the treadmill and trying the occasional class. I'm not sure we really accomplished a whole lot more than feeling the success of trying. Unfortunately she moved away part way through the year and without her there I felt no inkling to go back. I'm not sure why, but I just didn't.

So for me the road to fitness was not one I travelled alone.

That was until something changed. Another one of my friends decided to learn how to teach aerobics. I was a little shocked at this. First, that it would occur to her to do this and that she wanted to. I had never known her to enjoy working out although she had told me that she spent lots of time in the gym years before.

So in support of her, I got a membership at her new gym and started attending her class. She kicked my butt. There was no way I could keep up with her although it was fun trying. She had lots of enthusiasm and everyone loved her. It was fun to go to the gym and I found the classes were tons better than walking on a treadmill. Funny enough I also found I would work out a lot longer and quite a bit harder. It really didn't take long for me to start noticing changes in how I felt. Tone was slowly taking shape on my body. And things that I thought I was genetically stuck with seemed to offer hope of reshaping. I never knew that I would be able to change how I looked and like doing it. I had just been travelling down the wrong road of doubt and discouragement.

I never intended when I started working out to drop five sizes. But that's where the road led. I am grateful to have had friends to help me get started.

•••

Real friends are those, who when you've made a fool of yourself, don't feel that you've done a permanent job.

•••

http://bit.ly/mUs4Qw

3. IT AIN'T ABOUT THE FISH FOOD

Strategy: Count the cost.

I didn't know. Okay perhaps I didn't slow down enough to really count how much it was going to cost me. It sounded good. Free.

It was a free aquarium with several fish. Friends of the family were moving abroad and they needed a new home for their fish. They were happy to help us get the tank over to our place and educate us on how to care for the tank and the fish. They were even happier to know that the fish would be enjoyed and taken care of.

I thought the kids would enjoy the fish. They did. Then they lost interest and the fish blended into the background just as any picture on the wall.

It was all fine except then we started to realize how much it costs for the filters, the special chemicals and of course extra fish and toys we had to add to the tank. Beyond those things, the tank had to be cleaned and it wasn't a job I felt adept enough to do nor had any real desire to do. Clearly that had to take some extra cost to convince a certain kind husband to take care of that chore. And you know that when we get into the husband's currency sometimes that costs a lot more in the end than the few dollars for fish food.

I certainly didn't count the price that we would forever hear about how he gets stuck with the jobs no one else wants to do. I'm sure until he reads this he will have forgotten about the fish in the list. And I'm sure I'll have to pay admission to the "how you owe me" show once again.

How often do we pay much more for something free than we ever intended? How often do we say no to spending money on something that is just what we need because we think for some reason it's too expensive?

The couch costs way more than we recognize sometimes. Perhaps we think we are saving money by not going out and doing something. Perhaps we think we are too tired to go out. Not counting the true cost won't make the price tag any lower. The hidden costs of inactivity or avoiding the things we could do with our time is like buying a one way ticket in the wrong direction. Inactivity makes starting an activity harder. We all know that inactivity eventually causes health problems.

When we had had enough, we gifted our fishies to another willing family. Hopefully they got more out of those fish than we did. Would I have agreed to the fish tank knowing what it was going to cost me? Perhaps I would have redirected that money and energy into a different project. Next time maybe I'll count the cost behind what might be free.

••

Stupidity is forever; ignorance can be fixed.

••

http://bit.ly/ofQT9A

4. STARTING THE ENGINE

Strategy: Realize learning takes a lot sometimes

Like most people I was sixteen when I first learned to drive. I remember the first time I sat in the driver's seat and turned that ignition, foot too heavy on the gas the car roared. Oops! This was very exciting. I was about to be allowed to take this pile of metal onto the road even though it was not for any destination except getting some of the basics of driving.

Gas. Brake. Too much gas. Too much break. Too little gas. Too little break. This was worse than the bumper cars at an amusement park. I don't know. Will I ever get this? I'm sure all the neighbours were scared spitless. That was enough for one day. Dad, you drive home.

Day two which was a couple of weeks later, we got a little further. Over time my foot started to get the feel for those pedals although they usually erred on the side of lead versus light. Over time I figured out how to deal with the signs and the forks in the road. Eventually my parents even let me venture out with a friend and once I passed my driver's test, freedom!

What a strange feeling being able to go anywhere I wanted. What a strange feeling exploring and becoming more independent. I'm sure my poor mother could not stand me driving that car on my own. But she knew I had to learn how to do it and somehow she convinced herself that it was okay to let me go, lead foot and all.

How many of us, although we are on our own, still hear our mother's (or whomever) voice in our heads questioning ourselves, checking and rechecking our own abilities? Can do this, can't do that. The reality is we can't do most things. That is, until we try and try again and again. When I got behind the wheel of a car I couldn't do it. And I still couldn't do it for a significant number of tries. I was just fortunate enough to have someone beside me that would allow me to try.

Have you ever met anyone whose motto in life is "I can't do it."? To me that is the most frustrating thing if they stop there. It's obvious. Of course you can't. If you've never taught a class, of course you can't do it. If you've never lifted weights before, of course you can't do it. I can't lose weight. Absolutely impossible.

Not being able to do something is not the point. Just because you can't doesn't mean you will never be able to. If I stood on the outside of the car and just thought about how I wasn't going to be able to drive, I'd be riding a bus today. If I just got in the car and attempted to drive down the road right away I'd probably be missing a body part right now – or worse yet not living.

I see people all the time who tell me they want to lose weight or get in shape. It's almost like seeing them stand outside of the gym staring at it and convincing themselves they can't be fit. I wonder if anyone has ever studied how long someone has to think about going to a gym before they actually go in.

How long did you think about driving before it was time for you to try? I'm not sure there is ever a specific time limit that you should think about something before you do it. But one of the first steps is learning how to turn on the ignition or even opening the door of a gym.

Perhaps gyms should give lessons on how to open the door of the gym.

•••

This year's success was last year's impossibility.

•••

http://bit.ly/oNHMKD

5. HIT THE BALL TO ME!

Strategy: Practice to find confidence.

My two oldest girls play baseball and they play very well. Baseball for them has been something that they loved from the beginning and it was their idea to play. If my husband would have chosen a sport for them he would have picked basketball. Having said all that both of us have so much fun watching them play and succeed. My husband certainly has spent many hundreds – probably bordering on a thousand hours helping them learn this sport.

This last year we had the opportunity to take our eleven year old to Texas to play in a weekend tournament with a friend who had moved there. Even though it was a team she'd never played with in a different country she did extremely well. We watched her change over the weekend from the silent player to the one leading the bench in team cheers. Baseball was baseball and she figured out that her skills were transferable across the border.

This particular team had never progressed far enough in their previous tournaments to play on the second day of the tournament. This time they had a little more gas in their tank and were pushing through the second game on Sunday trying to advance a little further. It just so happened in extra innings their team was up by two runs and they were defending against two runners on base. For the baseball fans you'll understand that the tying run was on base and with only one out it was a precarious situation.

If you ask my daughter, "What were you thinking at this point while you were playing second?" she'll tell you, "I was thinking, hit the ball to me!"

I was astounded by this answer when I heard her say this. How does an eleven year old have such confidence to begin with? Why would she want such pressure? I would never have thought that if I were in her shoes.

As the game continued, the batter hit a fly ball towards right field. My daughter jumped up fully extended and snagged it, then instantly dove over to second to beat the runner back to the bag. Double play. Game over. They won!

We were ecstatic. That was worth the ticket to Texas!

By the end they had finished fifth out of twenty teams and the best thing was that we got to go home with an unforgettable story.

Hit the ball to me. That's called living on stage!

How does one learn how to live in order to say that, mean it and then prove it?

As a baseball mom I know that ability took hours of fielding practice, practice in the gym over the winter, extra coaching by experts, laundry, strategic purchases at the sporting goods stores and a whole lot of driving around southern Ontario. That confidence cost a lot both in terms of time and money.

She is nowhere near putting in her ten thousand hours it takes to become an expert; however she is certainly on the way. Perhaps she didn't know that when she was practicing it was putting her on a path towards that moment or any other successful play. But that's what it takes. It is about the behind the scenes work. No athlete will tell you otherwise.

If I want to say, "Hit the ball to me," mean it and then prove it, I've got to get off the couch and practice.

• •

A prudent man foresees the difficulties ahead and prepares for them. [Proverbs 22:3]

• •

http://bit.ly/qHEZHc

6. THE FEAR OF THE THIRD

Strategy: Fear the right stuff.

Has there ever been a time in your life when it seems that you know too many people that are critically ill or in a bad financial position? Whatever the bad news, you get depressed just thinking about life.

When you have experienced loss or a general hard time, you know how it feels when you see others in pain. Your empathy is so sharp you feel as if their bad news is yours.

In my experience, fear is sometimes a pretty strong result. Fear becomes a trap. Whether based in superstition or worry we fear doing something because of what might happen. We are melted into our couch and then frozen still. We fear failure and ironically fear success at the same time. "What ifs" bounce off the walls. If this, then that and that might mean change. We know things change but we'd prefer to be in control of that change ordering it up like the perfect meal from our favourite restaurant.

On this planet unfortunately it doesn't work that way.

One of the scariest times in my life happened when after we had lost my first child – a full-term stillbirth – we decided to have another baby and then another. It was when I was pregnant with the third baby that I got really scared. I knew what it was like to give birth and go home empty handed. I knew what it was like to give birth and feel the joy of a little bundle. It was during the third pregnancy that I was crystal clear on which outcome I preferred. I became very fearful that history would repeat itself the wrong way. The fear kept telling me, "You're going to lose this one too."

Although our third baby was beautiful and full of life right from day one, I emphatically promised myself and all those around that we were done. Our family was perfect with two girls. Really the fear had shut the door.

That was until enough time had passed and I found the fear was quieter than the desire to have one more child. Time did make a huge difference and although I knew the real risk of a pregnancy I felt the risk of life without one more brought out the willingness to try.

I'm sure everyone was surprised when we announced we were pregnant after a break of six years. However we all could not have been happier. And to this day the youngest holds a special place in everyone's heart. She is a blessing.

You have to fear the right stuff.

Figuring out what the right stuff is does take work and perhaps time. But without "going there" we can live myopically and develop unnecessary phobias or even unhealthy thought patterns. Like a hermit we think self-protection is the way to go. I've found that you always get better information from listening to the wise regularly. Nowhere have I found more wisdom than in the Bible. Nowhere do I find wiser people than those who don't just attend church but that actually follow the Way. The trick is that this takes time, regular thought and participation.

We can get off track instantly. We think we know the answer. We need direction outside of ourselves. I've found that people are willing to share more than we think. People need to help others and people need to accept help. Everyone wins when we get together to keep ourselves and each other on the right track. But it does mean that we regularly have to show up especially when we don't always feel like it.

• •

Don't be afraid to take a big step if it's required.
You can't cross a chasm in two small jumps.

• •

http://bit.ly/nXznD8

7. THE CRITIC TRAP

Strategy: Check your mirror.

One of my jobs is to teach fitness classes. I love it. I love everything about it. There is so much challenge in being steps ahead in your mind so that the cues come out at the right time to make everyone in the room move in the proper way.

I love the interaction and the coaching. Once in a while I come up with something pretty witty to say and it cracks me up to be in that moment.

That stage was not always so much fun for me. In fact when I first learned how to teach classes I worked at a gym where there was no actual stage. We all faced the same direction and I led with my back facing the crowd. The only way I knew if people were following was to watch them in the mirror.

When I changed fitness companies I found out that we had to teach facing the crowd on a stage. That was nerve wracking at the beginning. Besides trying to figure out that I had to tell people to go left if I wanted them to go to my right side, I had no choice but to realize that in fact all eyes were on me.

Making that transition from the front row to the stage is a huge step. I've recruited many people to give it a try. It is not easy!

When we are in the front row we can watch and think, "Wow that looks like fun! I could do that." We can even start to criticize the person at the front, "They didn't cue that at the right time."

"They need to work on their form."

"They are too serious."

Whether it's the front row in a fitness studio or in front of your large screen TV, it's always easier than being on the stage. It always looks easier than perhaps it is.

Now just because something is harder than it may appear doesn't mean I'm not recommending it. Actually I think everyone should explore the stage – but you may want to check your mirrors first. (The mirrors in the studio are not there for your hair, you know.)

When you are on your couch we don't always figure out how far you are from the stage so the criticism flows pretty quickly. It's not a bad idea to consider how far away you really are as long as you're willing to take the next step.

You have a perfect image of this if you've ever watched the auditions from American Idol. The nicest looking kid with the sweetest disposition approaches the judges and opens their mouth to sing. And in a nanosecond everyone involuntarily reaches to cover up their ears. How is it that they didn't know they couldn't sing? Did no one ever tell them? Did they ever consider that they may want to run it by some less famous judges that would tell them the truth before the entire nation got wind that their skill level leaves much to be desired?

Check your mirrors I tell you. Check your audio. But don't let it stop you if you still have work to do. I'm just suggesting go and do the work before you put yourself out there.

It is always obvious when people didn't put enough practice in. You can't hide it.

So if it's the stage you want to try, get yourself properly ready by putting in the time carefully to look in the mirror.

••

If you correct yourself, others won't have to.

••

http://bit.ly/o3zlmJ

8. TO SWING OR NOT TO SWING

Strategy: Be ready to take your own stage.

Girls rep softball gets pretty intense by age ten. A rep team means that the team represents a city and travels to play against other cities. When my oldest was at the age of ten, some of the fastest pitchers in the league were already pitching fifty miles an hour.

I had never faced a live pitcher at that speed before so just to give myself the experience I decided to try to hit against a pitching machine. I had to laugh at myself because although I tried my best I didn't even hit one ball.

These girls stand in the batter's box and have to make an almost instant decision if the incoming pitch is a ball or a strike. Then they have to decide if they like it and if they are going to swing. Minimally they would stand there for one pitch and watch it go by. That might be good or not so good. One pitch when she is up to bat either means she hits the ball or the ball hits her! If neither of those things happen, they keep going until they get three strikes or four balls whichever comes first.

The thing that never changes is that when a girl is up to bat, the ball is coming. The choice is what to do with that bat in her hand. Temptation, opportunity. Does she let that one go by because it is no good? Or does she swing? If she misses she gets another try. If she misses too often she sits down.

That home plate reminds me of the stage. We've got to step up to the plate and try. We've got to swing at the strikes if we want to hit the ball.

What are the strikes in your life? Is it choosing to help someone? Is it trying to make a dream or goal a reality? Is it big like a move or having a child? Is it smaller like painting a room or changing your hair colour?

Every day those choices come at us. Knowing where the strike zone is helps. When it comes to right or wrong, do we understand where the line is? When it comes to something that will help or hurt us in the long term, can we recognize it? Is this something we should let go or is it something we should take care of?

Even if the ball is coming in too fast, we can train ourselves how to time our swing better. We can get the bat off the shoulder and load. We can watch the pitcher let go of the ball but we've got to be ready. Whether we actually hit it may take practice.

Watching a strike go by might bring regret and a painful walk back to the dugout. Not swinging at a strike is anti-baseball. We hate to see anyone not swing when they are up.

Swing batter, swing!

You are on stage.

•••

It doesn't do a person any good to sit up and take notice if he keeps on sitting.

•••

http://bit.ly/nxtj16

9. GET ON THE RIGHT TRACK

Strategy: Clean the inside of the cup.

I was speaking with someone I know who is anorexic. This girl is lovely and before our very eyes we could see she was going downhill. What a struggle it was to figure out how to help and what to say to her.

After some pretty uncomfortable confrontations and lots of therapy and doctor supervision, this girl started to make a turn towards getting healthy again.

I asked her what she thought started this in the first place for her. She had told me that when she was about twelve, she wanted to be healthy. She started eating just vegetables and then that turned into strictly eating only three meals a day and then limiting her intake.

It was amazing to me that a child who had an acceptable goal of being healthy got so off track. Clearly her definition of being healthy was according to her own made up definition.

Something went terribly wrong somewhere.

I've often wondered when people tell me they need life balance if they actually understand what that is. Just like my friend you can want something that is acceptable but really not understand how to get there and then actually find yourself in a worse position than if you had never chased after that goal.

It's like working very hard to clean the outside of a dirty cup and completely ignoring the inside. You've got to get to the core.

Why do you want balance? Why do you want to be healthy? What is the point? If you chase after these things what makes you think you won't get it off kilter in some way?

If you ever try to balance on one foot you may find yourself wobbly and starting to lean to the left. If you then self-correct and lean to the right you may over or under correct and fall over completely. Tightening our core muscles help us to centralize the body weight and with the abs tucked in you will be much steadier on your feet.

Our spiritual life is our core. We must have that in shape to not be so wobbly in our life. How does one do that? Is it even possible? Where do you go?

How are you going to find that new innocence? Is it possible? If you don't, how far can you get?

Run after what's right. Seek wisdom. Get proper guidance. Work on the inside and set your goals accordingly. Hold on. Persevere in this learning. Throw out what is not right. Continually improve. You don't want to work for something in vain or work for something that is on the wrong track.

••

You are what you are when no one is around.

••

http://bit.ly/nzbilZ

10. DAISY PICKING DAYS

Strategy: Be all in.

If you've ever watched young kids play softball you've probably seen the kid on the team that just doesn't seem to care to try. Perhaps they're more interested in understanding the botany of left field or they are working on their Rembrandt reproductions in dirt.

From the sidelines it is very frustrating to watch sleeping softball players. No amount of cheering seems to wake them. Bribery sometimes works. "If you just swing the bat, honey, we can go for ice cream after the game."

Other kids can't seem to tame their intensity. If they could win the game by themselves they would. These kids take it personally when they don't win and it hurts a little more. There is intensity in every moment.

Whichever the case you may have been as a child, watching your own children can be like looking directly in a mirror – amazing features and awkward foibles wrapped into miniature versions of ourselves.

How often do we want our children just to go for it and be all in? It's so much harder to live all in than to tell someone to be all in. What would happen if your friends, your family, you were actually all in?

A loss stings less when you give it your best shot. Another statement that is easier said when there is risk to be taken. Risk is scary. I suppose if it wasn't we wouldn't label it as such.

The problem with living "all in" is the daily part. If you were all in yesterday it somehow doesn't seem to count today if you're back on the couch.

As you go through life and happen to see someone else daisy pick through life remind yourself to live every day to the full. As you instruct your children to go for it and give all they've got, listen to yourself.

I've often found myself trying to encourage others to press forward and then realized I had better listen up too. It does help to keep me honest when I preach the right stuff. I have to follow it if I know it to be true. As I help others I find that it helps me to follow through. If I ignore what I've just said, it numbs my conscience and is no good for anyone especially me.

We all have daisy picking days or moments. It's in our nature. We have to force ourselves to concentrate on the game. Head in it. We need to decide to live this way each day. We know we'll be more successful when we do.

••

Many have the right aim in life, but they never get around to pulling the trigger.

••

http://bit.ly/oZRAnO

11. PUT THE BUMPERS IN THE GUTTER

Strategy: Exercise the motivation muscle.

Have you ever seen kids cheat at the games they play? Hand a two year old a yo-yo and see what they do. They'll put it on their finger and bounce their hand up and down and say, "Look I do it!"

Or hand a five year old a bat and see how many times they call your perfectly placed pitch a ball.

But how successful would that child be at their birthday party at the bowling alley without bumpers put in the gutters?

Why do we tolerate such inadequacies? Such cheating? How embarrassing!

Without a relaxing of standards for kids, how would they ever be successful? Without a lowering of expectations, so to speak, these games would never be fun for anyone.

If we treat ourselves a bit like kids when we try something new we might go further. Our tendency is to have the adult eyes on ourselves even when we may be starting something just like a kid. If you treat your motivation to develop a skill like a muscle that needs to be strengthened you can learn how to keep going.

When I teach fitness classes I try to help new participants understand how to back off until they win a few successes.

One of the first things I encourage brand new exercisers to do is to march on the spot and watch. The purpose is to move, getting your heart and lungs to work hard. So what if you can't do all the moves? That's actually normal. Sometimes we need just to watch for a while before we attempt things. We can start to be successful if as we are watching, we are marching. This is the same strategy people use when they first start training to run – sometimes they go back and forth from running to walking and back to running again. It makes us stronger over time as long as we keep going.

Applying these tactics to other areas of life can also be effective. What about something as simple as organizing your house? That may sound simple to some but in my house my family can trash a perfectly picked up house in a matter of hours. If I were to look around the mess and say it's not a success until it's perfectly cleaned, I probably would never get started because it would be too daunting. I find if I organize one thing, I usually have energy to organize a second. Over time I can make headway as long as I don't start with an expectation of perfection. Like a muscle that gets stronger, motivation can grow with use but we may have to remove lofty standards to get ourselves to start.

Treat yourself with kid gloves when you need to. Be nice to yourself. You'll get much further that way.

....

*The best place to find a helping hand
is at the end of your own arm.*

....

http://bit.ly/ptWZeW

12. GETTING THE GET UP AND GO

Strategy: Get enough fuel

How do I get more energy? This question was thrown at me as we finished our class. I could tell this participant was forcing her arms and legs to keep moving to get through the tough bits of class. It surprised me a bit that she had such a hard time because she was a regular.

My best guess was that she just didn't fuel herself enough before class. It does make a difference what you eat before or after exercise. It's something you can research and get some tips and tricks to make a difference.

You need to get some good carbohydrates in you a couple of hours before a class for example. One hour is okay if it's not too much food; and liquid is probably a bit better at this point. But exercise without fuel is not a great idea.

After exercise it's critical to replenish. Always go for real food first but if you can't eat within that time frame, grab a protein bar or drink to help. Again be sure of proper portion sizes whatever you do.

What about your emotional health? Social? Spiritual?

Are you getting enough fuel?

Sometimes getting off the couch seems almost impossible if we've been there alone for a while. I know I get charged up when I spend time chatting with friends. It helps me to do better in the other parts of my life. When I'm on my own I do well for a while and then being alone can turn to apathy.

Spiritual stuff is key. Regular recharging is something we must have. And getting enough balance between head and heart is of utmost importance. I see too many people stuck on feeling spiritual stuff without engaging the head. The problem is that the feelings come and go and if we've only fueled the feelings, the feelings lead us right back away from anything spiritual. We've got to find a way to use the mind in our spiritual life. The brain is starving for spiritual fuel.

Spending time daily is needed. Spending time weekly is critical. If you do not know what your beliefs are, putting off figuring it out is not going to help you. You may have to talk with people you trust and respect. You may have to read something you wouldn't normally read. You definitely will have to step out of your comfort zone in some way. I'm not suggesting look into every crazy spiritual thing. Use your mind. Use your heart. Ask. Explore. Decide. Follow.

The get-up-and-go doesn't come naturally. We do have to put something in to be able to get out the energy. We do have to work at it to reap any benefits. But with enough fuel we feel better and have a better chance of crossing the finish line in one piece.

• •

Feed your faith, and your doubts will starve to death.

• •

http://bit.ly/oSt04L

13. JUST ADD WATER

Strategy: Follow a successful formula.

So when you buy pancake mix are you one of those people who look for the "just add water" or do you go for "add milk and eggs"? Everyone has their own theories on which batter tastes better. And I am not sure I even know the difference. The true test might be if you know how to make pancakes without a mix. Recipes exist somewhere but why bother.

I'm sold on pancake mixes. I don't know why. But it must be easier, right? Some other simple fixes I'm not as convinced. I am much more likely to make muffins from scratch than a mix. Again I don't know why other than I think they taste better that way.

Have you every missed a critical ingredient while baking? Skipping the baking soda is just not a good idea. Sure your creation might be edible but it might not be as enjoyable.

When you make the effort to exercise it would be nice to be able to "just add water." Nike® promotes that kind of thinking with their "Just do it" but really what does that mean? What if you are missing a critical ingredient? I'm sure you'd still get benefit from just doing it. But how many people do you know give up on exercise almost before they start because they don't like the "taste?"

A group exercise class when done well is the closest thing to a "just add water" recipe. You don't have to know what's in there as long as you follow along. It's really impressive when your workout is designed by world-class fitness leaders and delivered live in your neighbourhood gym.

Sure you can buy the latest DVD and exercise in the comfort of your own living room. But how many people have found that they can keep that up? There was one TV show I used to love to watch and I actually exercised to it. The instructor was engaging and it was just long enough for me to feel like I was doing something yet short enough for me to be able to get through it. But all my plans to keep up my new routine were short-lived. The most exercise I got was transporting the videos in a box when we moved.

Participation is the secret ingredient. Too little participation and your class will be flat and your abs not so much. If your movements are not to your best ability, your best will remain unknown.

Well-established, well-thought through classes challenge your physicality and inspire your participation. Any activity that inspires your participation will give you the best results.

So what brings inspiration? The answer varies with the individual. For some it's music. For some it's format. For some it's content. For some it's a favourite instructor. For some it's the other participants. And yet for others it's the colour of the walls. Some factors can make up for the lack of another but all of the elements need participation to bring the recipe together for a great result.

Find your successful recipe and add yourself to the mix! You'll love the results.

••

He who wants milk should not set himself in the middle of the pasture, waiting for a cow to back up to him.

••

http://bit.ly/pRYJqP

14. CARS AND TOYS

Strategy: Beware of atrophy and understand adaptation.

The body is an awesome machine. Sometimes it seems we think of our bodies more like the first car we ever owned. I remember one of the first cars I had when I was in university was a powder blue K-car. The most annoying thing about this car, besides breaking down every month was that it wouldn't start when it rained. We'd have to get a pencil and shove it in the carburetor while someone else fiddled with the right amount of gas, turning the ignition and trying not to flood it.

Sometimes it feels like are bodies are like that K-car. And after a certain point we feel like it's hopeless and we just need to lease a new machine. But one never knows what changes can actually happen with a little regular effort.

There is a technical acronym SAID that stands for "Specific Adaptation to Imposed Demands." This one always amazes me and sometimes I wish I had these features on my own car. Basically your body will adapt to what is required of it. If you ask it to lift a particular amount of weight a number of times and you expend all your energy to do so, your body actually goes into production of tearing down muscle to make room for more. Then the next time it'll be much better prepared to cope with such demands.

Can you imagine trying to put one extra person in your car and not having enough seats? The next day when you get into your car you are shocked to realize an additional seat is ready for your required carload. The car can't adapt but the body can.

Atrophy is the opposite; it basically means "use it or lose it." I try to use the principle of atrophy with my kids' toys. And I really, really wish this would be an added feature you could buy alongside any toy like an extended warranty. "If the child does not play with this toy for sixty consecutive days and/or the child's age surpasses the designated age listed on the box, this toy will disappear. You may or may not be informed of this process." Wouldn't that reduce the pile of toys that tend to accumulate over time!

Now when it comes to our bodies, we are not so happy with atrophying muscles. Have you ever thought something like, "I used to be able to do…?" But if you haven't kept up that activity, your body repurposes its resources. Just ask anyone who has been in a cast for six weeks. That six-week period may have been enough for the bone to heal itself but the muscles around it seem to just shrink in that short amount of time.

Before I started exercising and learning about exercise I felt very hopeless about fitness. I never understood these laws of nature that could be used as tools to help me feel better and bring me more success. I started exercising because I knew I probably should and was presented with the social opportunity. If my friend was going why wouldn't I go too? The day came when I was literally delighted when I found it physically easy to lift the vacuum or could carry both my kids who totaled fifty pounds up and down the stairs.

We keep going and it gets better. Degeneration is the natural consequence of stopping. The good news is you still have today to start again.

••

Behold the turtle. He makes progress only when he sticks his neck out. [James Bryant Conant]

••

http://bit.ly/pC1nhS

15. USING CARROTS

Strategy: Inspire others to help celebrate your success

When my older kids were young I ran a daycare from my home. It was a rare day that I didn't get a "laugh of the day" from the kids.

I had to laugh at myself when one day I was in the middle of teaching a fitness class and I was about to start a song called the "Party Track." It was time to introduce this part and I said, "Who's ready for the POTTY track?" What??? Potty training and teaching fitness… the worlds collided.

Over the years I have done a lot of potty training. I believe I have helped fourteen kids learn how to use the potty. I've learned a lot about teaching from training kids. Sometimes we have to stick with the training for a long while before we see the results. Sometimes a little celebration goes a long way.

We were working with one little boy who needed just a little more encouragement. I said to all the other kids, "If he goes to the potty you all get a popsicle."

The kids were surprised! They confirmed that they heard me correctly and then every couple of minutes I could hear them checking if the boy was ready to go to the potty. They'd sit with him and encourage him. They'd make faces to help him understand how to find the feeling. Never did they get mad at him or scold or make him feel badly. This was a new game and they felt empowered to help their little buddy.

You should have heard the celebration when he actually went. Everyone erupted and jumped up and down the hallway. As if I hadn't heard, some of them quickly came and found me to report on the success! Clearly they were happy for him. And the little extra reward for his friends didn't hurt. He felt so successful and was beaming not only because there was such a celebration but he knew he did it. It took almost no time to get rid of those diapers once and for all.

That might be something I should try again in another scenario. Reward my friends or family when I reach my goal. That's one way to get support, isn't it? It's not that people around us don't want us to reach our goal; it's just that there isn't necessarily motivation for them to help us. Perhaps we should put the carrot in front of our nose – perhaps it makes more sense to put the carrot in front of our friends.

Whatever the case, including others in our celebration is much more fun. How can I include my friends in my goals?

• •

No one can whistle a symphony.
It takes an orchestra to play it.

• •

http://bit.ly/qrcPuk

16. HURRICANES IN THE HOUSE

Strategy: Get the to do list right.

I don't know who said this but this is my next secret, "Good enough IS good enough."

Is everyone safe enough? Is everyone happy enough? Is everything clean enough? Did everyone eat and drink enough? Did we do enough? Did we sleep enough? Did we exercise enough?

Everything around us will not be perfect. We cannot create a perfect world. And if we are so focused on doing everything perfectly we will most certainly fail. This does not mean don't try. Of course we must try. But try within a strategy.

I can get into a cleaning frenzy where I would wash every surface and put every single thing in its place. Whenever I've gotten started and allowed myself to go I feel very satisfied at the end of the day. However I am spent. Done.

My family hates this actually. Usually I involve them in the task; however they do not have the stamina and certainly not the interest. So I've had to take a step back and try to figure out what is important. Is the fact that every single cupboard is perfectly organized more important than the fact that we had a nice meal together? Is the fact that there is no speck of dirt on the floors more important than we all were able to attend one of the girl's baseball games?

Although everything competes for your time, there is always something that can be pushed off until later and always something that takes priority at that moment. Although there is a "to do list" it isn't always a "to do now list." And the other things take the status of "enough" until they are promoted to "now."

When my kids were little and it was virtually impossible to contain the hurricane of two little ones I made a decision to be harder on my stuff than harder on the kids. That didn't mean we didn't make them clean up. It just meant that we tried to create a different balance of importance and consider primary expectations.

The "to do now list" is critical and must contain the basic principles and morals of life. Treat others as you want to be treated. Love your neighbour. Teach your children well. Take proper care of yourself (eat, sleep, exercise, learn). Be a good friend. Give to him who asks. Work hard.

Too often I hear, "I never have time for..." or "I'm too busy to..." Right. So what I hear is that those things never hit the "to do now list."

We know if you don't eat right, you won't live as long on average than those who do. So if you do it now, you'll more than likely get more time later and feel better too. Right? How many other things are like that in life?

How do I get the "to do now list" right? Now that is an important question!

••

This fast age seems more concerned about speed than direction.

••

http://bit.ly/pi5h7W

17. I NEED A COFFEE

Strategy: Don't exaggerate.

Some have asked if I eat whatever I want when I work out so much. The truth is sometimes yes but mostly no. It's much more important what I eat than how much. I have found that I really need to pay attention to eating enough protein especially after I work out. If I eat extra veggies or fruit then it's never a problem. Those foods offer good payoff for the calories. They make you feel full for a lot longer than a highly processed food.

Often we think we are really, really hungry when we are just hungry. I've seen lots of people work their buns off in the gym only to put them back on at the dinner table.

No food is forbidden to me but all food is not always beneficial. Sometimes you just want chocolate. But it really isn't a substitute for real food – just a nice treat now and again. If I eat chocolate every day, yep, I'll put on five pounds.

What is the benefit of becoming a chocoholic? Or even declaring that you are one? My stomach is not the master. But I need to feed my stomach to live. Do we not have a greater motivation for life than eating? Do we not have a greater motivation for exercise than eating? If we do not, then perhaps we should start looking.

What about this low/no-carbs thing? Yuck! That does not appeal to me! And your body needs carbs! But again extra carbs will show up on your body.

It's tough to balance the food and keep focused. But even as we try we've got to tell ourselves the truth. We must choose the correct words. We can't forget or be deceived by lies.

I need a coffee. I need a drink. I'm starving. You can't have a movie without popcorn.

Really?

We sometimes are not thinking about what the words mean. But words are powerful. Words affect us. When we label ourselves with these words are we setting ourselves up for failure? Or at the least creating an inability to change which is only in our minds?

Fake it until you make it. You may have heard that said. Within that concept we have to start thinking differently to change anything. One way we can think differently is to change how we express what we are and what we are able to do.

"I'd like a coffee", "Time to unwind" doesn't imply that you are an addict.

"I'm ready to eat!" is much more accurate.

And although the experience in the movie theatre does have popcorn you may just want to change the "have to have" rule once you figure out how many calories and sodium you will mindlessly ingest if you buy a bag.

Let's use accurate and helpful words to keep us moving in the right direction. It may be a little thing but little things can make the difference.

••

Even a little lie is dangerous; it deteriorates the conscience.
And the importance of conscience is eternal, like love.
[Pablo Casals]

••

http://bit.ly/ro6Me7

18. GOOD LEARNING FROM A BAD BOOK

Strategy: Keep the motivation in your court.

Someone asked me, "Name the top five things you need to do in order to write a book." How's that for being put on the spot! One of the things I answered was, "It's a good idea to read bad books."

What a crazy thing to say!

In my experience, when I have read a less-than-stellar book it has prompted more action than if the book had a perfect set of instructions. Sometimes books have great titles that make me pick them up off the shelf and when I get into them, it is so painful to even finish the book. They have nothing to say. I once bought a book that I was so excited to read – it was something about simplifying your life. However I grew more and more disappointed as I turned the pages. I wondered why on earth they had even titled the book the way they did because it made no sense to me. I can't even tell you why exactly the book missed but I can tell you it made me mad because I wasted my time on it.

I don't know if you've ever said, "Someone should write a better book than that!" Generally when that happens to me at some point I have to look in the mirror and say, "I should write a better book than that!"

I have heard good advice. I have heard advice that was just plain wrong. I have seen good teachers. I have seen ones that need more than a little work.

When you come across that less than perfect educator you have to decide what to do with that. Your natural reaction may be somewhere from blind acceptance to extreme skepticism. Wherever you start, a moment of discernment and/or a little analysis can prompt learning from the not so good instructor.

This kind of thinking doesn't allow someone to blame the teacher or create excuses to justify inactivity. It keeps the motivation out of the hands of others. It is harder. But you'll guarantee yourself the best lessons that way.

One of my favourite math teachers in high school was actually a bad teacher. She didn't know how to teach as crazy as that was. If the students didn't understand she would just get mad. I don't know why I liked her. I just did. Math was always my best subject so when I didn't understand what she was talking about I knew it wasn't me. I'd take the text book and read it over a few times. I'd take the problem and sit with it until it started to make sense and the mathematical patterns would start to show up.

I finally got the idea that I could turn around in my seat and teach the next person who also was lost. Pretty soon I found I could help those around me and they would come to me which was fun. The other thing that started happening was that I had to figure out how to explain it better than the teacher. That was a challenge I liked.

You can take the deficiencies of others and let them become your motivation.

•••

Learn from the mistakes of others.
You won't live long enough to make them all yourself.

•••

http://bit.ly/pK4jM9

19. POLISH THE SILVER

Strategy: Persevere by recognizing your own stage.

Have you ever taken a vacation and then found that it's extremely challenging to get back on the right track?

Two weeks of holidays away from teaching fitness usually makes me worry about coming back. It's like I've lost my cardio stamina in that short amount of time. As an instructor I feel it. I know it's a huge hurdle for those participants coming back after a break. Granted, for me it's my job, so there certainly is a foundation of motivation to get back into it.

When we start to find ourselves on a stage, it creates a kind of good pressure that can keep us on the right track. When we know people are watching we behave better. It's like there is a visual image of our conscience staring back at us. When we are on stage and we are not practicing what we preach we know that is hypocrisy and we really don't like how that feels. Unfortunately if we ignore our conscience and keep getting on that stage we can numb our conscience. That is so much worse.

Awareness of the power of the stage in our lives is a good one. If we struggle in one area we may need the accountability that the stage creates.

Perhaps the stage is something in your life that doesn't involve a platform or amplification. When people around us see and interact with us they do watch and the stage is more subtle. Perhaps it's how you react to a crisis. Perhaps it's how you deal with the dandelions on your lawn. Perhaps it's even your choice of shoe.

Recognizing that we are on stage can help us not go into road rage when someone cuts us off. It may not matter in the long term that you shouted at that inconsiderate driver. But perhaps your reaction taught your child to react poorly when another kid used their favourite toy car. It may be insignificant that you pulled all the weeds out of your garden; however, your beautiful flowers may have made someone's day as they drove by your place.

I have noticed that one's body adjusts very quickly to more or less activity. Sure it may not take long to feel like you've lost stamina, but it comes back and keeps improving if you keep pushing. The next time isn't as bad as the first time or first time back. A few times later it becomes much easier. Teaching has been something that has kept me on track with my fitness. Guaranteed I would have given up many times and had to restart many more times. That studio, mic and stage work for me.

Fewer than one in a hundred people are going to aspire to finding the fitness stage. But each one needs the accountability to themselves to keep the regular habit of exercise. In order for that to be the case we must have strategies to keep going even after a holiday or some other interruption.

I like this analogy. If some of your good silver becomes tarnished, do you throw it out? I don't think so. It may not look like silver. It may look blackened. But you know with a little effort you can polish it up and it's as beautiful as ever. You've got something valuable there – make it shine for all to see!

••

He who says the days of opportunity are over is copping out.

••

http://bit.ly/qgxCuO

20. USE THE FURNITURE PATH

Strategy: Take baby steps.

Have you ever watched a baby learn to walk? If you are ever fortunate enough to see a child on a daily basis while they are in this early stage, be prepared for an amazing process. It will all happen when the child is ready and not before. But when it happens, it happens fast. One day, you can't coax them into trying and the next day they are running, and running everywhere.

Perhaps you've seen a little one cruise around the furniture quite efficiently and then instantly drop to hands and knees as soon as the furniture path runs out. They seem to play that game for ages.

"Oh, just try it. You can do it." You egg them on. And you already know they could probably take at least half a step on their own and probably already have. You just didn't catch it. What makes them hesitant to try? You know if you push them too hard you risk that they are just going to sit down on the spot and cry, "I can't do it!" You are sure you can read the bubble above their head.

Or perhaps your kid is the one who just cannot stop once they've started. It doesn't matter to them that they can't do it. They're still going to do it, and do it full speed ahead. They skip walking altogether. Running is what they want to do. It's a good thing you've already padded the house in preparation because you know that outsiders would surely think you are a terrible parent letting the kid get so many scrapes and bruises at such a young age. But what are you going to do? There is just no stopping them.

Of course there are other kids that want to walk and insist on having someone or something there holding their hand. First it might be a parent's willing hand, then maybe a push along toy. When they hold on to something as simple as a blanket and are convinced it is holding them up and they are getting support from that you know this is not about physical ability.

In any case, these kids eventually do it. They figure it all out. They eventually figure out how to run and skip and jump. And unlike other stages of life, no one really cares that your kid was walking at eleven months versus thirteen months once they get to kindergarten. They don't earn themselves early entrance into the school program of their choice. They don't guarantee themselves a spot on the high school basketball team because they learned to jump sooner than the kid up the road.

Those baby steps remind me of when I attended a fitness class for the first time. The first time I attempted a step class I could not figure out how to do what seemed so natural to everyone else in the class. On the step, off the step, which way? Why did it have to be so complicated? I had been walking up steps for most of my life but none that made me feel so incredibly uncoordinated.

Beyond trying to get my feet to go in the right place and not miss the step altogether, it was painful. Why is it so hard to breathe? Why does my heart feel like it's about to jump out of my chest? Can my face turn any redder? I thought I was about to die.

Baby steps. Those first few steps are not just small but hard work and sometimes painful. Perhaps when it comes down to it if we viewed ourselves as a small child trying to take our first baby steps we wouldn't be so hard on ourselves. And when we fall or it hurts, we'd figure out how to baby ourselves for a moment.

••

Train up a child in the way he should go — and walk there yourself once in a while. [Josh Billings]

••

http://bit.ly/pbTSls

21. REACH AND RELAX

Strategy: Focus your energy efficiently.

The cabinets in my kitchen are extremely tall. They go almost all the way up to our nine foot ceilings. I'm sure they installed them a little high. I cannot reach the back of the second shelf without fully extending my entire body. It's a real dilemma when I want the raisins from the third shelf. Can I get any more length up on my tippy toes or lifting my shoulder or stretching the finger tips just a tiny bit more? Or am I going to have to go over and get the stool?

Another kitchen challenge I have is loosening the lid on a jar. Do you ever find yourself scrunching up your face as you try to undo the lid? All that energy put into the face, when you could put it into your grip?

How about you handy people? Have you ever seen someone take a hammer halfway up the handle and start nailing? I can see you watching in disbelief as they take four times the number of swings, or perhaps taps, they would need to if they had only used the handle properly and let the hammer actually do the work.

If you are running on a treadmill, what benefit is it to shrug your shoulders? None. That is counterproductive. The work should come from your legs and moving of your arms back and forth, not lifting the shoulders. Steadying the core also does help.

Is the wrong part of your body tense when you are trying to accomplish something? How is your technique? Have you got the right tool? Are you using leverage the best way possible? Are you trying in the right direction? Is there something you could be doing better?

No matter how much I stretch I can't get further than my 5 foot 4 frame will get me. No matter how much energy I put into my face, it won't make my grip stronger. I'd be able to run further if I didn't waste energy pulling my shoulders up to my ears. I wonder why these extraneous uses of energy are so natural? Whatever the challenge, the logical solution is often right there. A pause and realignment can save us that energy for the real task.

Our instincts can misdirect us. The goals are not impossible. However we can laser our energies in the right direction if we have the precise effort, the appropriate non-action, the right tool or assistance. Whether we are just getting off the couch or on the way to the stage we may need to focus the energy a little more resourcefully and stop doing stuff that doesn't really help us. Efficiency will help us get to the place we want to be sooner. Pause, realign and then go!

••

Do not mistake activity for achievement.

••

http://bit.ly/rqQMnU

22. GAZEBO WOES

Strategy: Keep at it.

It wasn't right. Something was amiss. We were trying to assemble our backyard gazebo tent and it was not the easiest of tasks. Where a normal backyard tent would be square or rectangle, we had chosen the one that had the curved roof and so not one angle was straight. We fought the wind. We struggled to line up all the parts correctly and screw it in so it was stable enough.

Finally we had got the structure up and the top cover was on. All I had to do was put the screen up.

Sounds easy enough. It took me more tries than I like to admit to get it right. I put the hooks on the lower rod. That was wrong. Then I put it on the upper rod which was right. However I had put it on the wrong side of the pole. Then I realized the outside was on the inside.

What do you do when you come across this kind of frustration?

You could ignore it and keep trying. You could take a break and come back to it later. You could ask someone to help you. You could sit there and look helpless until a helpful individual crosses your path.

Before declaring defeat how many strategies do you generally try? What if you tried just one more?

What if you did something to keep moving? Isn't that better than giving up?

I'm a big believer in taking active time outs. Not just a time out admitting defeat but a break where we come back to it a little later.

Sleeping on stuff really helps me. Somehow my brain keeps working subconsciously on the problem. Work problems, decorating dilemmas, even how to approach relationship issues sometimes need a little time. My conscious brain can get in the way at times and I end up just banging my head against a wall not being able to find a solution or even an approach.

As much as my gazebo is not really a "stage" the neighbours certainly have seen the structure jutting up above the fence. People see what you do. Perhaps the neighbours would not have noticed that it took me several tries to get my screen installed correctly. However what I do with my backyard is visible. My actions do speak. So if I needed any further motivation to finish my projects, remembering I'm on stage can help to keep me persevering even if I need a time out every once in a while.

· ·

Stopping at third base adds no more to the score than striking out.

· ·

http://bit.ly/pQocBS

23. JOURNEY OF A THOUSAND MILES

Strategy: Take one step at a time.

Have you ever used a pedometer? It's one of those little things that looks like a small pager and counts each step you take. You have to put it somewhere near your hip so it can register the impact you make each time you step.

Fitness experts tell us that we should accumulate ten thousand steps each day in order to keep us active and healthy. "Wow. That seems like such a lot of steps." I thought to myself. "Really? Every day? Ten thousand?"

So I put this thing on and spent my day as usual taking care of my kids, cleaning the house etc. At the end of the day I was pretty impressed at the number five thousand. Not bad. But not ten thousand either.

What happens when I go to the gym for a class? Another four thousand? Cool. That's much closer to the goal.

Over the next few weeks I started to take notice of the things that I did that added lots of steps. Walking to the bus stop to get the kids was a quick five hundred. Practicing new choreography for class easily boosted me way past the goal. I wondered how most people would find enough activity in their day to reach those numbers. We are generally not active enough and the lower pedometer reports are the reason.

One lady I met at the gym told me about her stamps. She had committed to herself that she would walk on the treadmill thirty minutes a day and when she did it, she gave herself a stamp on her page. She explained how satisfied she felt after a month of stamps and even though it was such a simple and small thing it helped to keep her on track.

When we move from the couch to the stage we really have to just take one step at a time and whether it's a number on a display screen or a stamp in our book we've got to figure out how to keep going no matter how far the stage is away. We love the feeling of reaching our goal but it's only reached by accomplishing the small daily actions.

It may seem kind of silly to set up a reward chart for yourself. That would be something to do for the kids, right? But if you still remember the stamp your grade two teacher had or the lick it and stick it gold star you go to put on the chore chart at home this may be something worth trying again.

••

Failure is the path of least persistence.

••

http://bit.ly/q8cfwn

24. AND ON THE SEVENTH DAY...

Strategy: Rest.

A nd on the seventh day God rested. You may not know this but it is a general recommendation for all to take a day off from exercise. Does that surprise you?

I think many people have trouble taking a day of rest. It actually wasn't that long ago that you couldn't find a store open on a Sunday. Now we are surprised when a store is not open. You can do anything you want on any day of the week pretty much.

I know I have had to work hard at organizing my schedule so that I don't have to work on a Sunday. It takes some effort to arrange to have that day off.

In my experience, when the experts say, "It is better if you..." they are more than likely right. In terms of rest how can we argue with the first example? And though my feelings at the time may not agree with the experts, it does me no good to go with my feelings.

I have found my body does a whole lot better with exercise on five or six days. I have more energy to do a better job when I've rested one day. It is generally known that you should not weight train two days in a row because your body needs time to rebuild the muscle that was worked. We do well with work. We do well with rest. We need a balance.

Balance does not come from feelings. If we try to balance on one foot and we feel like we are falling, we most certainly will tip over. But if we tame our feelings by focusing on a point on the horizon and keep our core tight, we most certainly will keep better balance on our foundation.

This is also true with life. When we focus on a true, unmovable point with our eyes and commit with our gut we will have much more success. If we focus on a point that shifts, so will we. If we relax the disciplines of life, we also feel tipsy.

What are the true points? What disciplines work?

I've heard that if you sleep in one day a week that will make you more tired the other days of the week which is just the opposite effect of why you would want to sleep in. Our feelings can get the better of us. Maintaining health habits for sleep and rest are important.

Creating schedules for our lives that give us the proper balance between rest, work and play is a basic building block. And we fight it when we should trust it.

••

Counting time is not so important as making time count.

••

http://bit.ly/q8cfwn

25. RAINBOW PROMISES

Strategy: Remember we are not in charge.

When I think of rainbows, I am reminded of children's pencils and books that have those colourful arches all over them. Sometimes tacky, kids are drawn to the colours. Perhaps it's because all the colours are there.

I remember as a kid playing with the water hose in the sun and being amazed at how little rainbows would appear if you got the angle just right.

Or what about that coffee table book that displayed pictures of perfect rainbows? So perfect it was hard to believe.

A couple of times in my life I have seen the perfect rainbow and been awestruck. Once when I was exiting a big box store, a perfect arch covered the entire city it seemed. I was amazed. But then I was also more amazed that not many around noticed it or stopped to take a look. To me it was an incredible picture of the busyness of life – all the cars, all the shopping – and yet above it all was this calm beautiful bow.

Was it that everyone was so busy? Was it that they had all seen many rainbows before? Or have they forgotten what a rainbow stands for.

When there is a great disaster people mourn over all that was theirs that made their house a home. Hurricanes, floods, tornadoes, earthquakes and their stuff is gone. Even worse a family member is lost.

As we watch the details in the news we feel sorry for these people and are thankful it's not us. We turn the TV off and continue on. But how are we confident it won't happen to us? Do others worry about this? Do people lose sleep over these risks? I don't know.

Science tells how the light is refracted and the colours separated into a rainbow through water. But why?

You can look at the initial historical event in the Bible and debate the historicity of the occurrence. You could even debate who the author of a book of the Bible is. You can argue about semantics or verbiage.

But what if these debates are potholes in the road that can set us off course? What if in the examination of the details we miss the grander plan?

Don't get me wrong – the details are important if not critical! But what if we don't successfully identify the right details? What if we don't step far enough back to see the full picture those mosaic details create?

We've got to stop and see the rainbow, remember the promise and take that into every day.

••

*Faith helps us to face the music,
even when we don't know the tune.*

••

http://bit.ly/q3Zemz

26. DON'T LOOK AT THE BALL

Strategy: Keep your eyes up.

Where do you look when you walk? Are you a feet watcher? Or do you look up?

My tendency is to look down and make sure I don't trip over my own feet. But if I think about it, I do know where my feet are. They are where they've always been – right underneath me. There's nothing I'm going to trip over. The floor is even. I have enough space. And yet somehow I don't trust myself.

If you look at someone else moving and watching their feet, you may notice that not only their eyes are down, but their neck curves forward and their shoulders round down. Not the most attractive position. In fact, it's not the most healthy posture.

Why is it not healthy? If you look at the side profile, you can see that the chest is compressed forward and those chest muscles are contracting. That means that the upper back muscles are fully relaxed. A significant imbalance can occur making our chest stronger than our back. Considering many of us use computers on a regular basis and tend to lean forward, we spend a lot of our time in incorrect posture.

When we go to use our back, perhaps even for an easy task, we can strain it or throw it out of whack because it is not as strong as it needs to be. If you have ever had trouble with your back, you know it affects everything – making moving very difficult and often affecting mood.

So how can we avoid back trouble? One answer is to train the back properly with moves you use on a daily basis. Good balance of your pelvis (not tipped forward, back or to either side) and correct alignment of your shoulder blades (together at the back and down) are great cues to start. If those two parts are in correct position, your spine will naturally follow a correct alignment.

Moreover, your eyes will naturally look straight ahead when your spine is in position – forward and not towards your feet. So remember to lift your eyes! Know where you are going, not just where you are.

When I was a kid learning how to throw a baseball, my Dad always told me, "Look where you want the ball to go. Don't look at the ball." And somehow when I did that it went where I wanted it to go more often than not.

Let's look up and be aware of our destination. Trust that your feet will do what it takes to get you there.

And besides people will appreciate seeing your eyes up!

••

*He who doesn't know where he is going
may miss it when he gets there.*

••

http://bit.ly/nmfGpS

27. THE MOTIVATION MUSCLE

Strategy: Don't wait for motivation.

So how does one get motivated? Tough question. And perhaps if you spend too much time on answering this question, you might not DO anything.

Until you are fully and perfectly motivated, you cannot have success. Right?

Good thing you are smarter than that. Of course motivation helps, but it's not necessary. Doing something is always better than not doing something. We can only build motivation the same way as we build muscle. And if you wait for your muscle to appear before you lift weights, you will be waiting an awfully long time.

For the past number of years I have been trying to figure out how to eat more healthily. I can't say I've been particularly motivated to actually change how I eat. But one think I decided to do was to start watching the Food Network. I found that by watching people prepare food it was pretty interesting. Before I knew it I was writing a grocery list of new things I had to pick up. Into the kitchen I would go armed with a scribbled down recipe.

After a year or so of experimenting with these recipes and different ingredients I certainly felt more comfortable in the kitchen and found I was able to whip up some great meals with more healthy ingredients.

My motivation muscle has been exercised. I might even consider researching more healthy diets and trying something else new. I think I could now handle it.

So you don't feel like going to the gym. You are not motivated to move. You can't stand the treadmill. The classes are too hard. Good. Uh huh. Yep. That's right. I see.

Does that all really matter? You still have to do something. So do it. It doesn't exactly matter what it is as long as you are moving. And you won't love it until you do.

Can I tell you one more secret? The only reason I exercise as much as I do is because of others. If people show up to my class, I will teach it for them. And who knew I would gain so much from doing that.

••

Do something. Either lead, follow or get out of the way.
[Ted Turner]

••

http://bit.ly/p1POi7

28. OPENING THE GYM DOOR

Strategy: Find the why of your stage.

I have heard a few people say, "The best part of the gym is leaving." It seemed strange to me although I'm sure I felt somewhat similar at the beginning but can we do better than like leaving?

"I'm going to keep going to the gym so I can beat my body into submission." Hmmm. That doesn't sound like fun. Okay maybe it is for someone needing an outlet for their self-hatred.

"I'm going to keep going to the gym so I can brag about my membership." Fine, but is that all it's good for? Having a membership means nothing if you don't show up.

"I'm going to keep going to the gym so I can lose weight." That might work if you do something about the eating part too.

"I'm going to keep going to the gym so I can tone my body." Why? "To look good." For what reason? "To find someone." That might work if you find someone who loves you just for your shape and you keep your motivation to keep your shape and your someone. But I've found that life is not usually simple as that.

"I'm going to keep going to the gym so I can feel strong and have more energy." This is a pretty good reason in terms of the length of time that you can feel the benefits throughout your day. But when is it good enough? How strong is strong enough? And what happens when you reach enough? Do you stop? Or do you keep going to maintain. Again maintain for what?

"I'm going to keep going to the gym so I can hang out with people." That is one of the most rewarding parts of working out with someone. You get to know that person. But what happens when your friend loses motivation or their life changes? How many gym friends have you had? I know I've had many.

"I'm going to keep going to the gym to...." Well I'm not sure how you finish this statement but perhaps we shouldn't finish it too quickly or we will finish going to the gym too quickly.

Motivation comes and motivation goes if it is not a lasting motivation. I started my fitness journey for different motivations than I continue with. I wonder if I will always continue with fitness. I hope I will. I trust I will. I will set my life up so that I can. There never is enough time for everything in life. Things must come and go. But if there is motivation towards fitness, it must be something that can carry forward.

"I love to lead people. I love to work with people. I love to be warm with people. I love to be physically strong to be able to help people do what they need to do. I love to be fit enough to be playful with my kids. I love to be physically quick. I love to be physically able to do hard tasks on my own. I love to see people have their own success. I love to cheer others on. I love to have energy through my day. I love to have a physical stress relief. I love to have time on my own. I love a mental and physical challenge. I love to feel success in leading, inspiring, teaching. I love teaching. I love performing. I love having the microphone."

That is a lot of "I love's." I'm kind of surprised there are so many things that I've been able to list. And it's no wonder that I love getting on that studio stage in the gym. If there is a different stage that can give me all of those things perhaps I'll switch to it. But for now, to the gym I go. If you can give me all of those things perhaps I'll switch to it. But for now, to the gym I go.

••

If you see a turtle on a stump,
you know he didn't get there by himself.

••

http://bit.ly/olVwia

29. TRIPLE SPILL

Strategy: Persevere even when it's a mess.

It was a job that allowed me to be at home with my kids when they were little. I operated a home daycare. It was chaos. But it was fun.

At one point I had Nathaniel age three, Kirsten age one, Amelia age one and Brook also one. These were my full time kids while the older ones were at school. Children and parents were arriving, other kids were leaving to the bus stop with one of my helpers and the little ones were having some breakfast. You can picture the chaos.

Once this morning rush was over and we were just about ready to start the day's activities, I would sit myself down with a cup of coffee and take a breath. This was not only enjoyable but really necessary for me to gather up enough energy to tackle the day.

On this particular day, I had one in the high chair and I was carrying my coffee to go and sit down. It was not to be. I heard the orange juice spill in the kitchen and simultaneously realized that Nathaniel was attempting to go potty and he had accidentally peed on the floor.

So I quickly set my coffee down on a small table in the hallway and ran to help. When I glanced back I saw Kristen grab my hot coffee, attempt to drink it and being shocked dumped it all over her.

I'm not one of those who believe things happen in threes. However we may want to enter this story into evidence for the case.

Immediately Kristen, the coffee taster, got the attention and luckily she was okay and could wait for a wardrobe change. Then before anyone could find their way to splash in the bathroom puddles I took care of that mess.

High chairs are great because no matter how much noise the kid makes they are locked in and safe when you need them to be. Finally the orange juice was addressed.

At that point all I could do was laugh and make a note to myself it would probably be best to invest in some more paper towels. In fact perhaps consider buying stock in the paper towel company.

I like to remember the craziness of this day. But more than that I did survive that day and others like it. Sometimes people would comment to me that they don't know how I "do it." Perhaps at the moment I wondered the same thing.

• •

You can tell when you're on the right road — it's all uphill

• •

http://bit.ly/pjfH7G

30. MIND REHEARSALS

Strategy: Find ways to practice.

Business school was one constant group project after the other. Generally the final product ended up as a presentation in front of the whole class. That was another challenge that I immediately started to worm my way out of. Still to this day if I ever have to do group work, I avoid being the note taker and I avoid being the presenter.

I am a thinker-talker not a writer-presenter when it comes to group work. If I'm going to speak about something, I have to know what I'm talking about and have had the time to put a lot of thought into it. Presenting others' ideas is tough for me. Writing while I'm thinking and others are discussing is not one of my multi-tasking strengths.

I learned this the hard way. Some of the other students had previously heard me speak at some point in business school. I was eloquent and held the crowd's attention on some topic. I was prepared. So when this particular group work was complete, the group started to discuss who would take the lead in presenting. Unfortunately I was nominated and couldn't get out of it.

What happened next was probably one of the worst moments on stage at business school for me. I tripped over every word and could barely make the group's points. As I tried to keep going, I couldn't find my groove. What was so bad was that the whole group was relying on me and I couldn't pull it off because I freaked out.

Again I had to learn a lesson here. I wouldn't do that to another group. Frankly this group would never let me do that to them again either! So I decided I had to rehearse even if it were in my head a few minutes before I had to speak. I would play with how the words would sound and how I could get my point across.

The thing that I've noticed is that over time I have had to rehearse less for short presentations and do a fairly good job on the fly. For bigger presentations I still talk my way through the presentation in my head. The nights before those presentations I toss and turn in bed as I try to fall asleep thinking through my words. It may be an unconventional way to prepare but I feel much more prepared and calm when it's time to take the stage.

I love to work with the audience and I love to get interaction. But that was not always the case and for me the trick is always in the preparation. Preparation can be for the one presentation but preparation is layered over our lifetime. We can see ourselves improve and change as we continue to take the stage.

• •

Success is sweet, but its secret is sweat.

• •

http://bit.ly/oiJ0zY

31. I WAS THE QUEEN OF EXCUSES
Strategy: Little by little.

I knew I should, but didn't. The thought would hit me; maybe, one day – nah, I'll do it later. And there I sat on the couch. My reaction to the internal prompting was to agree it was a good idea to exercise but then let the thought go by. I suppose it wasn't an extensive list of excuses but a very convenient one. I was not terribly fat – but neither was I fit. It wasn't that I couldn't move, I just didn't feel like it.

I still dragged my heels when a couple of my friends wanted to get fit. But I was running out of "cop outs." I knew they weren't going to accept any of the excuses I was tempted to verbalize.

One day my friend thought it would be a good idea to go out in the evening for ten kilometer walks around the neighbourhood. I couldn't imagine walking ten K. That was something one did for a walk-a-thon when you were a kid in school. However I knew it would be socially more painful to refuse than physically painful to go. My only excuse was actually on the side of action! I didn't want to miss the fun of chatting and the quiet of a nightly walk was appealing. My hips ached, my feet ached, I could barely keep up to the quick pace that was necessary but when we were home I felt like I had accomplished something.

Shortly after that my friend shocked me by telling me she was going to teach fitness classes. Pardon me? Again, I had no real excuse – I had to be a good friend and support her so I went to her class. At least she would make it fun. She did, even though I thought I was going to die with my heart pounding out of my chest.

That was my start towards fitness. Little did I know at the time my excuses for laziness were changing into excuses for becoming fit. How did that happen?

The behaviour change was not overnight. But little by little the excuses made me step forward. Little by little it became easier on my body and my heart and I liked how I felt. I also was stunned how my body was changing. It wasn't my plan to go from a size twelve to a two. It wasn't a goal to be fifteen pounds lighter than I had ever been in my adult life. But I sure liked it!

By doing one thing I liked, I discovered more and more benefits. My daily chores weren't so difficult. I could lift without straining, I could work longer. I could go further.

Little by little the time in the gym also became more enjoyable and the sweat pouring off me didn't seem like such an inconvenience but a cleansing reward for showing up and moving.

• •

No one ever climbed a hill just by looking at it.

• •

http://bit.ly/qa0wkn

32. IT'S NOT JUST ABOUT THE SCALE

Strategy: Know your measurements.

Have you ever experienced someone else noticing your progress before you do?

I notice that people who regularly take my classes change. All of a sudden it seems they are smaller in one way or another. No, it's not everybody nor every week. But once in a while, I look to the front left corner or wherever where so-and-so usually stands and why yes, they definitely have lost some weight.

Sometimes I'm so impressed that I blurt out in front of the whole class, "Wow, you're looking smaller!" And depending on if that makes you more proud than embarrassed you'll be feeling taller too. (My sincere apologies to those who I've said that to who feel more embarrassed! But I feel so proud of you – and of me too!)

I have also noticed when I do comment either during or after the class the participant says, "Oh I don't know if I've lost anything really." And I think, "Look at yourself, you are definitely smaller!"

Perhaps you are measuring your success using only one form of measurement – one number that doesn't move very much. You know what I'm talking about— the scale.

In addition to the scale you should also measure your body fat percentage and lean body mass. These numbers will probably move before the scale will move. If you are adding any muscle mass, your muscles will weigh more than your fat. You can talk to any personal trainer to help you do this.

One of the best things to do is to take measurements of your body. You may notice your clothes fitting you differently but taking actual measurements will give you a number to compare.

And best of all, take a picture! You need a GOOD bad picture of yourself. A good before picture is one which you would be willing to show people how much you've changed. Too often we have only BAD bad pictures that we've already destroyed because they are too embarrassing. So get yourself together and take a picture. You'll be so happy to see your progress.

Most of all KEEP these numbers and pictures so you can refer back – a quick glance back will keep you going forward! Keep showing up, keep trying a little harder each time and you will keep seeing some change. If you feel you can't see the change go right back to your measurements and see for sure. My guess is there will be improvement.

•••

If God can make penicillin out of moldy bread,
he can make something out of you.

•••

http://bit.ly/qaYnV3

33. MAMA NEEDS A NEW PAIR OF SHOES!

Strategy: Start with the foundation.

She said, "My feet hurt; do you think I need new shoes? What kind would you recommend?"

A well-engineered shoe will make a complete difference to how you feel during and after your workout. If your shoes are old you may notice a few more aches and pains in your joints or the bottoms of your feet might hurt.

Be prepared to spend money. Well-engineered shoes are not cheap. They put tons into research and development and the details of the shoes are there for a reason. I heard that one pair of shoes can pass through three hundred pairs of hands in its manufacturing. Yikes!

Get the right kind of shoe. If you are doing your sport quite often (three times a week for example) you probably need to find a shoe specific to that kind of sport. Cross-trainers or an aerobic shoe gives support while you move forward, back and side to side. Running or walking shoes are great for forward motion.

Don't be shocked that your shoes wear out before they look worn out.

My shoes never seem to look old but the bottoms of my feet and my joints certainly know that I need to go shopping again. Apparently shoes last for only a specific number of miles that you go.

Get some help with finding the right fit and it will probably save you some time. The sales staff should be able to look at how you walk and how the shoe fits to help steer you in the right direction. Ask around for stores that have a great reputation for spending time helping their customers. But basically the shoe should feel good as soon as you put it on. If it doesn't, try a different kind.

Whatever the shoe, it should not be an excuse. It is a tool. If it makes you go further towards your goal then consider it.

I feel that good workout clothes make a difference to our workout. Clothes that do not breathe feel heavy and hot. Loose fitting clothes can sometimes rub the wrong way making the work more uncomfortable than they should be.

It is not necessary to have all the latest and greatest but if it's a tool that will help you accomplish your goal and keep you from getting stuck go for it. Be comfortable while you do your good work.

••

There are no shortcuts to any place worth going.

••

http://bit.ly/pOLAL9

34. LESSONS FROM POTTY TRAINING

Strategy: Recognize sometimes there are a lot of steps to learning.

I hate to bring up the subject of potty training again. However I have learned a few lessons from this parenting course. Whether you have ever been involved in the process going through it with a toddler, potty training is one of the hardest things to teach a child. And yet as a parent it's also one of the most exciting steps when you no longer have to change dirty diapers. Indulge me a bit here. As I mentioned before, I can actually say I've potty trained about fourteen children in my years of motherhood and baby sitting. In fact, I feel more pride about that than I do for some of my other accomplishments. What other thing can make a grown adult basically do back flips down the hallway?

Okay so why potty training? Well, it is training. It does take a significant amount of time. And most of all there are many, many more steps to it than people realize. As adults it just makes sense to go into the bathroom and go, right? Wrong. So wrong. Did you know there are about thirteen steps the kid has to figure out just to pee in the right place? Let's see if I can list them for you.

Feel the need. Hold it and keep holding it until step thirteen. Realize the need is felt. Identify something needs to happen. Call for help. Go towards the bathroom. Open the bathroom door. Go in.

Take pants down (which may or may not have several associate steps to do with buttons and zippers). Take underwear down. Get on potty. Aim into potty. Actually pee.

Thirteen steps! Plus all the next steps after the task is accomplished. We ask these kids to go from knowing step one and step thirteen to adding the rest of the steps. So how fast do we want them to perfect steps two through twelve? How fast can they get it?

Timing definitely is a key point. People talk about kids being ready to toilet train. What does that mean? Are they ready to do step one through thirteen? Absolutely not. They can't.

How are you going to know when they are ready? Ready for what? Well if this was a completely different task, say for instance helping someone attend a gym, when are they ready? We might say they are ready when they open the door and walk through. But really most people can't. And frankly there is no acknowledgment that there are even other steps they should do before they swing the door on its hinges with the purpose of doing something inside the building.

Forgive me for the analogy but picture the kid who is toilet training. That toilet is a pretty scary thing. You are asking them to balance their bottoms on cold porcelain while naked and aim their pee into a puddle of water. How is this better than peeing into a nice soft cloth that sucks the moisture away from their bottoms wherever they happen to be at whatever time they feel the need?

You don't feel afraid of the toilet now, do you? Something you did so long ago is second nature. Perhaps next time you are about to learn something new you can remember yourself as a little toddler and know that you'll get it. You just need to learn all the steps and do it over and over and sometimes over again until you get it.

•••

By perseverance, the snail reached the ark.
[Charles Spurgeon]

•••

http://bit.ly/qTcKA2

35. PUSHING TO FIND PURPOSE

Strategy: Have a purpose.

What is your purpose? And when you know that does it give you motivation?

If you answer that your purpose of exercising is "because I know I should" or "I paid all this money and I don't want it to go to waste", you need to keep thinking. Those kinds of answers might be reasons but they are not purposes.

Purpose needs to be a little deeper than that. If you know you should exercise, great. But why? Because you want to be healthier? But why? You want to be healthier to be able to play actively with your grandchildren? Okay, that's a purpose. It's for your grandchildren and you. I think you'll appreciate that and so will they!

You don't want to waste the money you've spent on the gym. Sure that's an admirable reason. But why? You could have spent that five hundred dollars on Botox? Well, sure but if you want to go that route I'm sure you'll find that money somewhere to do that too.

Not wasting money is a tough one. It's avoiding a guilty feeling. That guilt is helpful and should be used to get you on the right track. But the trouble is, if you keep ignoring that guilty feeling, over time you can get used to it and find that you no longer really feel guilty about it. But if we take that negative reason and turn it towards something, we will feel more encouragement to get to our goal.

What is your direction? What is your purpose? Does that help to keep you motivated?

My purpose has always been to help others. As an instructor I love to teach and to encourage so others can feel great about themselves and live their life in a stronger manner. I also help others become instructors because that helps influence even more people.

One day I found myself helping my parents move about 1000 slate tiles that were going to be laid in their house. I found that I could move quickly and easily lifting and moving these boxes to where they needed to go. I found my heart rate went to that familiar rate as it would while I was lifting weights and I started to have a bit of fun with the rhythm of back and forth.

It was a new way to help others for me. I was physically able to do a practical job that was needed. That was a new benefit that never occurred to me that I would experience. I sure liked being able to help that way!

••

It's nice to know that when you help someone up a hill you're a little closer to the top yourself.

••

http://bit.ly/pTxMAX

36. TAKING THE FITNESS STAGE

Strategy: Give to receive.

When I took my first class, I loved it! I saw how we could get a whole body workout within the class and that made sense to me. I felt the challenge of the cardio and the muscle conditioning and it wasn't so impossible. The class made me smile! And that smile got me the job of becoming an instructor! It was another excuse to keep moving. I had to practice if I wanted to teach and that made me move all the more. To get others to move properly, I had to move properly. To motivate others I had to find motivation. And all of these things just kept giving back to me.

My husband started noticing that my posture had improved and in fact I literally grew one half inch taller than I had been in my whole life. How was that possible? My upper and lower body certainly toned. I added muscle which made my body look much smaller. My core strengthened. My behaviour changes resulted in physical changes and attitude changes.

My body started to prefer movement instead of the couch. The aches and pains I had felt for years in my neck and knees which I had regularly experienced were forgotten.

Fitness was a regular part of my life, two and three times a week. The baby sitter relied on my needing her to watch the kids while I was at the gym. The people in my classes relied on me to help motivate them. And my body relied on the conditioning to be able to accomplish the other tasks in my life. Fitness was a winning combination.

These days I see the look in some of my participants' eyes. They wish they could be me. They wish they could look like I do and accomplish what I do. They don't realize that they are doing it and they are becoming their own change.

If I try to explain where I was they don't always see it. Sometimes I'll pull out an old picture of myself to show them. At first they don't realize it's me and then the light goes on. "If she can do that, maybe there is hope for me." You can set a new direction and line up excuses to support action instead of passivity. Decisions happen one at a time and the results are at a pace that is attainable even though challenging. Long lasting behaviour change comes little by little. With the fuel of behaviour change we no longer hover like a helicopter; we accelerate forward like a jet. These behaviour changes may start physically or mentally but both are affected. And these lessons learned in the gym will affect the other parts of our lives – well worth the investment!

• •

Thinking well is wise; planning well is wiser; doing well is wisest of all.

• •

http://bit.ly/mViXtb

37. DOUBLE LUNG TRANSPLANT AND STILL GOING

Strategy: Always be thankful.

She was in my class a few weeks before we started to get to know one another a little. A lovely lady that once in a while showed up with her husband. I didn't really notice anything different about her other than she was a small lady that tried hard.

One day she shared with me that she had undergone a double lung transplant. I didn't even know that was possible – let alone possible to heal well enough to exercise in a fitness class.

She explained how hard it was and how painful it had been. But just looking at her at the time was an inspiration.

Another friendly member who loved the classes would seek out her favourite instructors to make sure she didn't miss a class. I knew she had some health problems and that her doctor had recommended she start exercising. She was quite well known to the instructors and we loved having her in class.

One day I learned that the lady had experienced a heart attack. The doctors told her after the fact that if she had not been so fit she would have likely died from the heart attack. Her husband took the time to say a special thank you to one of the instructors who went to visit. It was because she loved the classes and took inspiration to exercise he still had his wife.

Every once in a while we hear stories like this at the gym. I am so grateful that we have the opportunity to help and give people more life or a healthier life.

Sometimes we forget that life is short. Sometimes we forget that right living is important. When you are faced with a tragedy or even stories like these we can be shocked or even depressed. Choosing to be thankful may not be the first reaction but it is a powerful emotion that we can develop when we reflect on these things. We can pause and realign our lives towards a better goal.

Exercise is not the be all and end all; however having a few extra days in this world is an amazing gift for ourselves and others. Living with gratitude is always a better way. Seeing what is good and lovely even in the hard times can make a difference to how we feel and then how we choose to move forward.

What things are you grateful for? What can you be thankful for even when everything goes wrong?

••

Look backward with gratitude and forward with confidence.

••

http://bit.ly/nQC7wq

38. HOW DO I GET RID OF THIS?

Strategy: Balance satisfaction with dissatisfaction.

How do I get rid of this? (Ask this question while pinching the sides of your waist.)

I had two different people at two different times come and ask me the exact same question last week. Even though these ladies looked lovely to me, they were not happy with that extra five to ten pounds they have resting around their mid-section.

Unfortunately I wasn't one hundred percent sure what to tell each of them. The diet that was described to me didn't sound off-base. I certainly noticed they were regular attendees to my one class so it looks like they have been working hard enough. I wondered if they were being hard on themselves. I wondered if they didn't like the process we are all in – aging. I wondered if they were paying a little too much attention to some of those people who try to sell us this or that magic pill and/or this or that new life changing program.

When you watch a show like America's Got Talent each contestant is looking for a bigger stage where they will be discovered and magically whisked off into a lavish life where everyone knows their name.

Sometimes it's really clear that that person is never going to be successful on such a stage. You wonder if they have been living in a bubble where no one told them the truth of how their so called talents actually stack up. I often wonder why so many desire such a stage and if it is really what they want.

Stages we see on TV may not be the reality for us. They may not even be good for us. Finding the stage that fits and where we are satisfied is thrilling. Whether your audience is one or one million there will always be a mirror to look in at the end of the day. Whether you put the work into your body or something else it will never be perfect or complete. But I do believe putting the work in is one thing we can be proud of. Knowing we are taking the stage in our own life by living today as we should, that is the real show.

Why do you need to have a perfect body? Do you have to have a huge audience? Dreams are awesome but check in with reality to see if your dreams should be fine-tuned. We all can keep working on that.

•••

Success comes in cans; failure comes in can'ts.

•••

http://bit.ly/o4P5MB

39. PARTICIPATION OBSTACLES

Strategy: Take small steps and build a little courage.

Twenty per cent of my grade was based on participation. That was a huge challenge for me in one of my first business classes at university. It scared me half to death.

The room was set up in a u-shape, like bleachers equipped with desks. We had to set up a tent card displaying our name. The professor held the lectern in the centre and could see everyone. In fact, everyone could see everyone. There was no hiding.

So started the discussions. I can't even remember a single thing that we discussed because I was very worried about how I was going to participate. I didn't even know what I thought or if I even had an opinion about any of it. We had just embarked on the first term of business.

About the second or third day of class I started to notice that each time someone made a point the professor would make a mark on his page. I decided that if I were to have any chance I would have to try to say one thing every session. It would be my goal to form my words into understandable sentences and logical thoughts.

I would concentrate very hard on the conversation. I would try and come up with something I could add. It was so much work.

Part way through the course we were able to check in with the professor and see where we stood with our mark. I found out that my strategy was working. I certainly had enough points that my participation would be respectable.

Showing up was good but getting involved proved to be better. I had to look for opportunities to be able to raise my hand and offer something. I would never guarantee that what I said was an insightful revelation. I'm sure most of the time it was probably drivel. But I made it through.

All eyes were on me for that brief moment when the professor gave the nod to me with hand raised to go ahead and speak. I started to be okay with it towards the end of the course. Definitely I didn't feel comfortable and my heart would pound wildly each time I would think about raising my hand. However my face stopped turning bright red every time I opened my mouth. My voice started to find somewhat of a steadiness. I do remember I ended up with a B+ in the class and that was just fine with me.

• •

Falling down doesn't make you a failure, but staying down does.

• •

http://bit.ly/ppOjtF

40. PLEASE DON'T MAKE ME CHANGE!

Strategy: Accept change.

But I don't like change! How do you respond when there is a change. I already know that some of you love it and some of you not so much. That's life, isn't it.

Some of us like the new and different and others of us much prefer the familiar. If you liked the change right away – good for you. If you didn't – good for you; you'll like it just as soon as you get used to it.

In my job, I schedule many fitness classes. Sometimes I have to make changes to a popular class to make room for another class. Or sometimes the instructor is no longer available and we need to find a new instructor or a new class. As you can imagine sometimes the members are not happy to see that there is a change. We do know that it upsets their schedule sometimes. At the same time it does create an opportunity to try something new. We love it when members discover that they also love that new class. It rejuvenates them and reintroduces muscles that perhaps they forgot they had!

Did you know that you can't feel your muscles atrophy? Atrophy is a wasting or decrease in size of a body organ, tissue, or part owing to disease, injury, or lack of use. You may feel sluggish over time but it really is unrecognizable at the moment of atrophy. Your body just allows the muscles not to be regenerated because they are not needed.

This is what happens to us as we age and believe that we can't do something because we are getting too old. In fact your muscles do not know how old they are. All they know is activity or inactivity.

You do feel the building of muscle in something called lactic acid (creating that burning sensation that makes you want to stop). You also notice when your fitness level is being challenged. Your heart is beating fast; you start sweating and perhaps even go red in the face.

This is the part people don't like especially at the beginning. The body objects to this tearing down. When we experience the lactic acid we want to immediately stop because we think we are getting injured.

Maintenance may be somewhere in between but few of us are on that pinnacle of success where we never need to tune up just a bit more. So the choices can be narrowed down to two: change or atrophy.

So let's keep at it! And as our world changes around us, let's continue to make good choices where we do not give up.

••

It is better for you to wear out than to rust out.

••

http://bit.ly/oC4E0s

41. I NEED NEW KNEES!

Strategy: Find resources to help.

My mom's knees are not good. It is a common problem. In fact women are two to eight times more likely to have certain kinds of knee problems than men. Any time you have issues with a major joint that can arrest major parts of your life if you let it.

I am not an orthopedic student or a doctor so if you have serious problems you need to talk to the medical professionals. But I will give you my tips and tricks for your knees that you can try. I have noticed that when it comes to your knees, technique is everything.

Align your knees properly! Make sure your knees are pointing in exactly the same direction as your toes, specifically your knee lines up with your second toe. Never let your knees pass in front of your toes. They should remain directly above your ankle when you are in a weight bearing portion of the move.

Keep your weight in your heels! Whatever your activity you need your weight to be travelling from your knee directly down (vertically not on an angle) into your heel not resting in your toes.

Squats, lunges are your critical moves to keep your alignment. With all moves onto a step you must roll heel to toe, step off toe to heel. Focus on getting this part perfect before you attempt any propulsion into your moves. Pay extra attention to where your knees go in taichi or yoga strength moves. When walking, make your heel touch the ground first then roll your foot to your toe.

Take smaller movements until you are sure! If you are not sure you've got it correctly, don't go as low into your moves. Strengthen slowly. If you take your squat only to about twenty percent of your ability but you do it correctly, it will be better than if you push in the wrong direction.

Check your mirrors! Remember, those mirrors in the gym are not for your hair they are critical for you to see that you are getting it right. If you are not sure, get someone to check your technique before or after class.

Perhaps a knee problem is not an obstacle you face; however I'm sure you'll run into an obstacle that comes between you and your goal. In this case I have had experience helping some people with knee issues. In your case there will be someone you can find or some resource available to help you find your way through.

• •

When everything seems to be going against you, remember that the airplane takes off against the wind, not with it.

• •

http://bit.ly/pnY4PX

42. FREAKISHLY LONG ARMS

Strategy: Keep your story real.

Have you ever heard someone say, "I'm chunky?" "I don't like to run." "I am not coordinated."

One of my girls has in the past described herself as having freakishly long arms. I've never heard something as ridiculous. Her arms are perfectly in proportion to the rest of her body which also happens to be long and lean. I can't even tell you why she thought that about herself and of course I argued with her about it trying to convince her to change her mind. I must have somewhat won because I haven't heard that recently.

What's your story? Will your story fly on your stage? Is that something that people want to hear? Is it even true?

I have heard many statements made by people that cause me to think to myself, "That's not true. That's a judgment about themselves that really isn't a permanent thing. They could change that. Or that's just their perception of it and they have no clue." Clearly I'm not recommending that someone go around making statements to pretend they currently are their future perfect self.

Reflect on your stories and figure out if they are true. Your story does have to be natural to you. What is the purpose of your story? Are you reaffirming yourself? Are you inspiring someone else? Or are you attempting to devalue yourself in some backwards attempt to make others feel better about themselves. It doesn't really work that way, does it? All you get is pity. That helps no one.

Describe yourself in a few words. Brevity is a great asset. You want them to be drawn to you instead of looking at you as the "high and mighty." If the person is interested you'll know it and be able to explain appropriately. Carefully avoid buzzwords and speak in regular language so the listener can relate to you.

Keeping your stories real is endearing. It is also a critical foundation to building any relationship. So go ahead and share – give some information and ask for information. But do it kindly and truthfully; you cannot go wrong with that strategy. How you treat yourself shows others how you will treat them. Go ahead with a sense of humour about yourself but do it in love.

••

Humour isn't just a joke now and then; it's a basic survival tool.

••

http://bit.ly/qiW3gy

43. DOUBLE STROLLER CHALLENGE

Strategy: Know how to get strong.

When my kids were little we had to invest in a double stroller to get ourselves to the park. Little did I know at the time that after baby number two I would have such a workout opportunity. Pushing a heavy stroller increases heart rate and creates great resistance training for butt and legs. The glutes have to fire to push the two precious kids uphill. Maintaining control on the downhill requires core stability.

I didn't realize that when I went to the store to pick up a few things the milk and apples I added to the basket in the bottom of the stroller helped me burn more calories on the way back home.

I'm sure most moms can relate to taking the walk a little further because someone fell asleep and to stop would mean the quiet was over.

That double stroller helped me to start back on my fitness and all I thought I was doing was taking my kids for a walk.

Managing my girls' baseball schedule is the thing that feels like pushing uphill these days. Anyone who has a child play a rep sport or have their schedule dictated by all the activities their children are involved in may understand.

Knowing where to be and when, making sure they have all their equipment and water bottles, figuring out how to feed the family before we need to leave without relying on a drive thru is a major challenge. Night after night becomes the marathon. By the time I actually get to the events I'm ready to collapse into my folding chair – that is if I remember to put it in the trunk of the car.

It is crazy how one part of life does seem to train us for the next and it never seems to get easier. There are never fewer things to do. If you happen to be done all your projects, come hang out with me some time because I can always use more help!

Sometimes the challenges we find ourselves in, where we feel like we are pushing a Mack truck uphill, is just the thing that builds a muscle or helps to train us to persevere. This is one of the things I like about training in the gym. There is a mental challenge to push through while your body is on fire. I figure that mental strength does have the potential to transfer to other parts of life.

Whether we are raising children, cleaning our house or involved in a major project at work, mental strength can make a difference.

• •

When confronted with a Goliath-size problem, which way do you respond — "He's too big to hit," or, like David, "He's too big to miss"?

• •

http://bit.ly/rb1Pgp

44. MULLIGAN LESSONS

Strategy: Be in view of others.

I'm not a golfer. I'd love to be and I think I'd like it. In fact I used to own a set of golf clubs before someone stole them from our garage. My husband enjoys golfing and had bought a used set for me but it was such a challenge to find the time and someone willing to baby sit two young children.

But the few times I did go there was one thing I learned. Mulligan. A do-over. During a social game if there is a really bad shot that player is permitted to retake the shot. I'm sure there are formal rules as to how often this is allowed.

Knowing there is such a rule to allow you to try the shot again – how great is that? But really it is not an unlimited thing or what would be the point in keeping score.

My guess is a foursome shoots a lot fewer mulligans than the lone golfer. How could you ever trust the count of someone playing on their own? There is no witness to the actual number of swings. It seems to me that when we think we are alone that's where the real work comes out. If you can do it alone – you'll do it in front of others. If you cannot do it alone it'll be real tough to do it with an audience.

It's great training to be what you want to be when you are alone. Too often we let ourselves off the hook when we are alone.

How many people grab an extra handful of cereal or chocolate and munch away when no one is watching. Perhaps it doesn't even reach the conscious level of our brain however when someone is looking we tend to behave better. These actions eventually become visible over time, don't they?

Hiring a personal trainer is one of the things you buy to watch you, not counting any of the other benefits they may bring. They are your audience and you've paid a good amount of money for them to watch you. Clearly they are taking care of you ensuring you are doing the exercise properly. But they also keep you honest and push you to do better just by watching.

Some of the weight loss programs you can get involved in have this similar affect. You pay people to look at your scale every week. The scale doesn't lie. Neither can you imagine a different number on the scale when someone is there to record it for you.

Everyone needs a good friend or many good friends that notice when things are on track or starting to veer. Protect your friendships and do the work to be visible. When you can't seem to find someone available, don't hesitate to hire someone to help!

• •

Cooperation will solve many problems. Even freckles would be a nice tan if they would get together.

• •

http://bit.ly/oypOCM

45. DESTINED TO FAIL?

Strategy: Label well.

Destiny is predetermined; it is usually inevitable or irresistible. Failure is an insufficiency. It falls short. It doesn't perform what is required or expected.

Sometimes we like to state our predictions about people – especially little children. We see their failure and their deficiencies and declare them to be permanent.

You can't. You won't. You aren't.

To say otherwise would be impossible. To declare the opposite would be untrue.

Could a five year old amount to anything if a teacher told him he was not a good student? Would a student who struggled with math in grade school ever be able to teach fractions as an adult? What about the girl who loved to paint but was told she wasn't very artistic by her grade two teacher? Would she ever pick up a brush? How could a girl who warms the bench on the high school basketball team ever become a leader in physical activity?

But what if? What if it isn't about natural talent? What if failure and hopelessness leads to eventual success? What if there is something called development? What if learning is possible? Is anyone destined to fail? Or is the destiny in the trying?

What was set in the mind of the five year old was only undone when the boy was in his twenties when he realized he was wasting what talents he did have. Over the years he has become an innovator, someone self-taught in the technology arena, an expert communicator.

The boy not good at math had several teachers who believed in him and with those rays of hope he continued to try. He, himself became one of the most popular teachers in school. He led many teams to win championships in basketball and volleyball, initiated an amazing annual talent show, but was an incredible math teacher who could understand how difficult math was for some kids. And if they were willing to try he would help them also understand the math.

The girl, who loved to paint, stretched herself to go to university for art. She found after years of leaving the brushes on the shelf she still loves to paint and in fact has sold many paintings, showing her work in multiple venues admired by many.

The girl who warmed the bench, got off the couch as an adult and started taking classes. She learned how to teach and now has led thousands in her fitness classes and managed hundreds of other instructors in Canada's largest fitness company.

You can. You will. You are.

• •

Quite a few people owe their success to advice they didn't take.

• •

http://bit.ly/oig0Ai

46. HOW TO LOOK GOOD - PREGNANT!

Strategy: Shine yourself up.

I found myself pregnant for the fourth time. Okay, it was not a surprise. But a seven year break between kids, we often faced the unspoken question with a raised eyebrow. And I wondered – am I crazy? Funny how life evolves.

I spent several years stating that I was done and any future children would be adopted. I had got my "baby fix" from taking care of many children in my home daycare. Really all of those kids I cared for were mine for the time the parents lent them to me. We had tons of fun together – even though it was often chaotic!

As life changes, my children and the other kids I had been watching were getting older requiring less full-time care. The choices were to find some younger children to keep the daycare family going or to move on to other things. It was in one of these moments of contemplation I had the opportunity for a full-time position outside the home. I decided to take it and my daycare and the effects on the house were dismantled. Good-byes were said. Toys were given away. Baby stuff was dispersed. That chapter done. Or so I thought.

Almost a year later the topic came up again between my husband and me – time for a permanent decision. Were we done or not? Don't think too long! And yes we decided to go for it one more time.

"You look so good!"

I was five months pregnant. Hearing that you look good when you are starting to grow feels great – even if they are lying! But if you think about it what pregnant lady doesn't look fabulous? When you are pregnant, everything is changing and unfamiliar. It's not the easiest thing to think or feel that you do look fabulous! Perhaps many women struggle with this kind of thought even when they are not pregnant.

Taking the time to exercise, eat well, sleep and drink lots of water is a simple formula. It's not really harder than that to feel your best no matter the situation – even though you may not feel like it. Shining yourself on the outside makes all the difference to how it feels on the inside. Taking the simple steps to keep the discipline of the basic requirements of life will make all the difference. One foot in front of the other.

Taking those few steps over a pregnancy is a great foundation. It doesn't stop when baby arrives. We still have to keep that simple formula. The only thing is now we have to teach the little one the same rules.

Whether you have ever been pregnant or ever will be it always feels better to look good.

• •

He who wants to move mountains
starts by carrying away small stones.

• •

http://bit.ly/ogDMLY

47. THE PEN IS MIGHTIER THAN THE SWORD

Strategy: Write it down for success.

Everyone has their own set of goals and dreams they would like to reach. With the myriad of strategies, have you considered using something as simple as a pen (or some other handy note-taking technology)? If the pen is truly mightier than the sword, why not use it to help win the battle?

The discipline of note-taking can help keep us on track and serve as a motivation to strive a little further. More than just pen on paper, we benefit from the self-evaluation that occurs as we jot down our progress.

Whatever the target, journaling the progress can help to keep the focus. If we are to look at healthy living there are a few ways to view it.

Cardio diary: Track the number of minutes you are active in the day. It counts if you do shorter bursts of activity! It counts if you do it all at once in your day. Compare week to week and note where you may be able to increase your activity. A little extra will make the difference over time.

Pedometer steps: Write down the number of steps your pedometer records. Do you get to the recommended daily amount of ten thousand? How close can you get? Perhaps you will be surprised to see how few or how many steps you actually do. By writing this down you will create a history of your progress and a vision for your future.

Workout log: Persevere with recording how much you lift in the weight room. If you enjoy competition, compete against your own numbers week by week. Do one more rep. Do one more pound. Compete against yourself and you win.

Food Journal: Eating without awareness of the volume of food or the number of calories is a huge trap. When you log your food intake, you hold yourself accountable for each bite. A food journal is a great way to make you aware of the cost and benefit of each food item. This self-guided education is invaluable in helping to develop healthy eating habits.

Water Intake Monitor: Sometimes the simplest solutions are the easiest to forget. Making sure you drink enough water throughout the day has lots of benefits to your health. Write it down to ensure you are taking in enough. Remember to increase water intake with increased activity.

Flexibility Notes: Many people do not know that you can improve flexibility. It is more challenging to quantify flexibility but it is possible. Even if you note how you feel, you will be able to see changes and progress with effort.

Body Measurements: The circumference of arms, thighs, waistline, hips, chest are excellent benchmarks for progress. We often see changes in size before we see the numbers move on the scale.

Whether you choose to track many details or just a specific few, the activity of regular journaling is an excellent method for self-evaluation and self-motivation. Be as complete as you like. Make it a habit. Review your notes regularly. Observe how your notes help you succeed in reaching your goals!

• •

Hope is putting faith to work when doubting would be easier.

• •

http://bit.ly/qaUUqY

48. TURNING UP THE HEAT

Strategy: Train for it.

To change the shape of metal, you have to turn up the heat. Our bodies are kind of like metal that way. Turning up the heat in terms of a workout means that we increase the requirements on our cardiovascular system. Quite simply cardio-vascular refers to heart and lungs. If you increase the amount of work your body is doing the cells in your muscles need more oxygen to do the work. More oxygen has to come through the lungs and into the circulatory system. So we start breathing more quickly. To get that oxygen there quicker, the heart has to work faster which means an increased heart rate.

So why do we want the cardiovascular system to work harder? First and foremost when we ask our bodies to do something that it isn't used to doing, our bodies respond. Amazingly and over time the heart chambers actual grow in size when we become fitter. If the heart can take in and send out more blood each time it pumps, it has to pump fewer beats per minute.

The average person's heart beats seventy-two times per minute. But the fitter person's heart beats fewer times. So if we can save our heart ten beats every minute, that certainly should be a plus in terms of benefits of improving our fitness level.

So how much work do we have to do to make a difference? Well enough for our bodies to get the message that it's not as efficient as needed and should adjust accordingly.

Here's a question. If you could improve your cardiovascular system, what kind of activity do you want to be able to do better? Some people may want to improve their speed and power on the basketball court. That takes fits and stops. So training should be in line with that. Interval training is a great way to improve your ability. Interval training is where you have high activity for a certain length of time and lower activity, generally called recovery, for the next length of time. Repeat the cycle as many times as you need. Intervals could be thirty seconds or five minutes or any other length of time. When we suddenly need lots of energy to do an activity but we don't have to do that activity for an extended period of time, this is a great training method.

In your daily life do you ever feel like you are trying to gasp for air just because you are so busy? Whatever you are trying to accomplish why not try training to push a little further to get to your stage. It might mean strategically choosing to do something hard that you wouldn't normally do. I am always impressed with those who go out of their way to take a course or learn something new. It pushes their system and trains them to be able to handle more. And though they might feel like their brain got the benefit of learning, I imagine there was also some reorganizing of the schedule even to allow that time to be taken. That is a challenge too!

What should train for? If you train, you'll be much closer than if you just collapse on the couch in defeat.

• •

A wise man is like a tack —
sharp and pointed in the right direction.

• •

http://bit.ly/nVYveO

49. TEN WAY TO GO'S!
Strategy: Celebrate success.

E very single effort in the gym is a step forward to better fitness. And when you add up all the little improvements, you eventually get big success. But sometimes that success is a long time coming. How can you keep motivated to stick with it? One strategy is to celebrate along the way. When the finish line seems distant, use small successes to keep yourself on track! Here are examples of ten successes worth celebrating.

You lasted five minutes longer on a cardio machine: Five minutes may not seem like a lot but five minutes a week times twelve weeks can get you to a whole hour! Why wait to celebrate the difference between fifty and sixty minutes. Start with the difference between five and ten, ten and fifteen and so on. If you keep adding five, you will still get there!

You fine-tuned your technique: When you perfect a squat or other muscle move, you avoid injury and get the most out of your workout. That's efficient and effective!

You improved your flexibility: The fact that you can touch your toes is a big deal if you never could before! Stretching is a skill. Pat yourself on the back for those little changes.

You changed your attitude toward exercise: I used to think "_____" now I do "_____." Listen to what you are saying and note how it has changed. You may be trying to lose weight so you look better. But people will certainly notice your change in attitude much sooner!

Your energy has increased: You feel better when you exercise and you are better able to take on daily challenges. That is a life change. Keep reminding yourself of this success – it'll help you keep going.

You met new people at the gym: Don't under estimate the power of friends at the gym. They will give you an excuse to go!

You understand more about how to move: Education sticks with you and that head knowledge helps when you don't feel like trying. If your motivation is all about your feelings you are missing a critical foundation and will fail. Learn and you are building a stronger foundation to your fitness. Isn't that more important than a short-term goal?

You are able to converse during exercise: This is a sign of improved fitness. When we are working at our maximum it is very difficult to talk but as you improve your fitness level you may be surprised that you are able to talk where you couldn't before. Now that's one of the first steps to becoming an instructor!

You feel more comfortable with the equipment: We are creatures of habit and we like what we know. If you are feeling more comfortable at the gym in the surroundings and know what you should be doing, you are less likely to quit this wonderful new habit.

You exercise regularly at the gym: Regularity is much more important. It will keep you fit for life – a relatively healthier and longer life!

So go ahead and recognize yourself for these achievements! Feel good about your small successes. Keep moving forward and you will have big success to celebrate!

••

Enthusiasm is the best protection in any situation.

••

http://bit.ly/pHomI4

50. UP AND DOWN

Strategy: Be okay with the cows and bees.

What happens when you reach a dream or a goal? Say you lose fifty pounds or climb a mountain or even have a child. Perhaps it's been a journey you've been on for a very long time and reaching the goal is like you reaching the land of milk and honey.

I had a friend who did lose fifty pounds. This was a huge amount of work for her. She spent so much time exercising on her treadmill and lifting weights. She learned how to instruct fitness classes. She watched everything she ate, counting calories and balancing her nutrition. We celebrated all her hard work and cheered her on with pride.

As she got smaller and stronger she looked great. She felt great too in terms of her accomplishment. However she was a little surprised at how else she felt. She had envisioned she would be happy. But she didn't find that. She found that she was still herself – just less of herself.

I'm not sure what was so different for her at the new weight. However the expectation may have been that the weight loss would solve her problems. On the contrary, it just changed the types of problems she had. Yes she looked great and physically felt great but that too made her think differently about what clothes she would wear, how to do her hair and how people responded to her. You can't have milk without cows or honey without bees. She had to learn how to be okay with the cows and bees.

In my friend's case I think she really didn't like the newness associated with her new life. What was comfortable before was no longer comfortable and she wanted to go back to the way things were. She didn't end up keeping the weight off and added a protective layer back in a relatively short amount of time.

I wonder if those suddenly jettisoned into fame are surprised when they get what they wished for. You can't have milk and honey without poop and buzz. I imagine there might be a lot of that.

The new normal is another way to think of it. What used to be normal, the way I did things on the couch cannot go with me into the future. New vocabulary has to include, "I used to…" We have to stop doing the things that held us back. We must hold on to the new way. Eventually that new way will be comfortable but not until you get used to it. Looking back is tempting but if looking back turns to longing for the way things were, watch out! It's too easy to go back.

• •

He who wants to make a place in the sun should expect blisters.

• •

http://bit.ly/ofb6O6

51. YOUR DESTINY

Strategy: Take the next step in obedience.

Have you ever wondered if there is a special place for you in this universe? Have you wondered if at some point you will meet a certain place in time and space in which you were born for such a time as this? Is there is a specific stage that has your name in lights flashing above it waiting for your arrival?

My Dad has said lots of things that have stuck with me and that I quote on a regular basis. One of the recent things he said was, "Your destiny is to take the next step in obedience."

Really this sums up how to get "from the couch to the stage."

I don't know if I or anyone else has a specific job that we were put on this earth to do. Even if that is true, how are we going to know when it has happened?

I suppose when our days our done we can only hope that we found those moments on our very own stage. And really who is going to say on their last day, "I didn't spend enough time on the couch. I wish I wasted away more of my days."?

That being said, all we can do is take the next step.

Looking too far down the road sometimes is overwhelming and encourages you to sit right back down. If you get up off the couch thinking you will run a marathon, I'd bet you'll find yourself back on the couch before the forty-two kilometers are ever run.

Taking the wrong next step is perfectly possible. Another thing my Dad says is, "It's never the wrong thing to do the right thing." That sums up the obedience part of his first quote.

I don't think people like that word obedience. It sounds old fashioned. That is until you become the parent or the boss and want to be obeyed.

Sometimes we want to know why or how but we can't always know that. We like to figure it out and when we can't it bothers us. I just have to follow the rules. Although that might be hard it does make life easier. When we get to be a parent or a teacher we can see that for the students.

Yet we still want it our way all the time, don't we? We want to know our destiny, when we will find it and we want to get there in our own way and right away. Too bad it doesn't work like that.

That next step in obedience – I think my Dad is on the right track. He is further down the road and may have an edge. Perhaps I'll just listen to his advice and see where it takes me.

•••

The cost of obedience is nothing compared with the cost of disobedience.

•••

http://bit.ly/mQVzxR

I will continue to share my life because that is good for me. I hope it is good for you too.

  To the stage I go.

••

Courage is being the only one who knows you're afraid.

••

http://bit.ly/pYhiIS

52. THE HUMBLE GUITAR

Strategy: Do it afraid.

I taught myself how to play the guitar. Well actually I should say I played around with my guitar long enough that it started to sound like music. I had taken years of piano lessons – some of which were pure torture and some not so bad. When my husband decided he wanted to learn the guitar I had a bit of a musical foundation to be able to offer some music advice. But once the guitar was in the house it was a challenge for me to play it.

Three chords were all we needed for a song. Good rhythm to strum was key. I played around with it and kept playing. It was fun but my fingers hurt!

As time went on, a friend and I started to write music. She was in charge of the music and I took the lead on the lyrics. What an amazing feeling it was to mesh the two together to put across the message we wanted to say. We thought we were on to something and looked forward to being able to take the stage to share what we had created.

We had the opportunity to perform and teach others this music which was well received. I couldn't believe I was playing the guitar and singing at the same time shortly after I had just learned to strum some chords. It wasn't great. But it wasn't too bad. I had to do it afraid. I had to do it even though I was nervous because my message was too important not to sing.

In many ways when I think back on this I am still embarrassed that it was only kind of okay. But I had to get on the stage. Every week I got on the stage to lead. Over time the people who joined me on stage came and went but I needed every single one of them to help me keep going and keep performing.

When a true musician would join me I started to believe even more that it was possible to sound good. When I was on my own it was tough to know that everyone could hear every mistake I made. Without those mistakes I wouldn't get better. Without trying I would still be playing to myself, message hidden away in my brain or just bouncing off the walls of my living room.

I still hesitate to call myself a musician just as I find it hard to call myself an athlete or even a writer. I suppose if I keep doing it those feelings of nervous hesitation will slowly melt into quiet confidence. I trust.

Proof

Made in the USA
Charleston, SC
29 November 2011